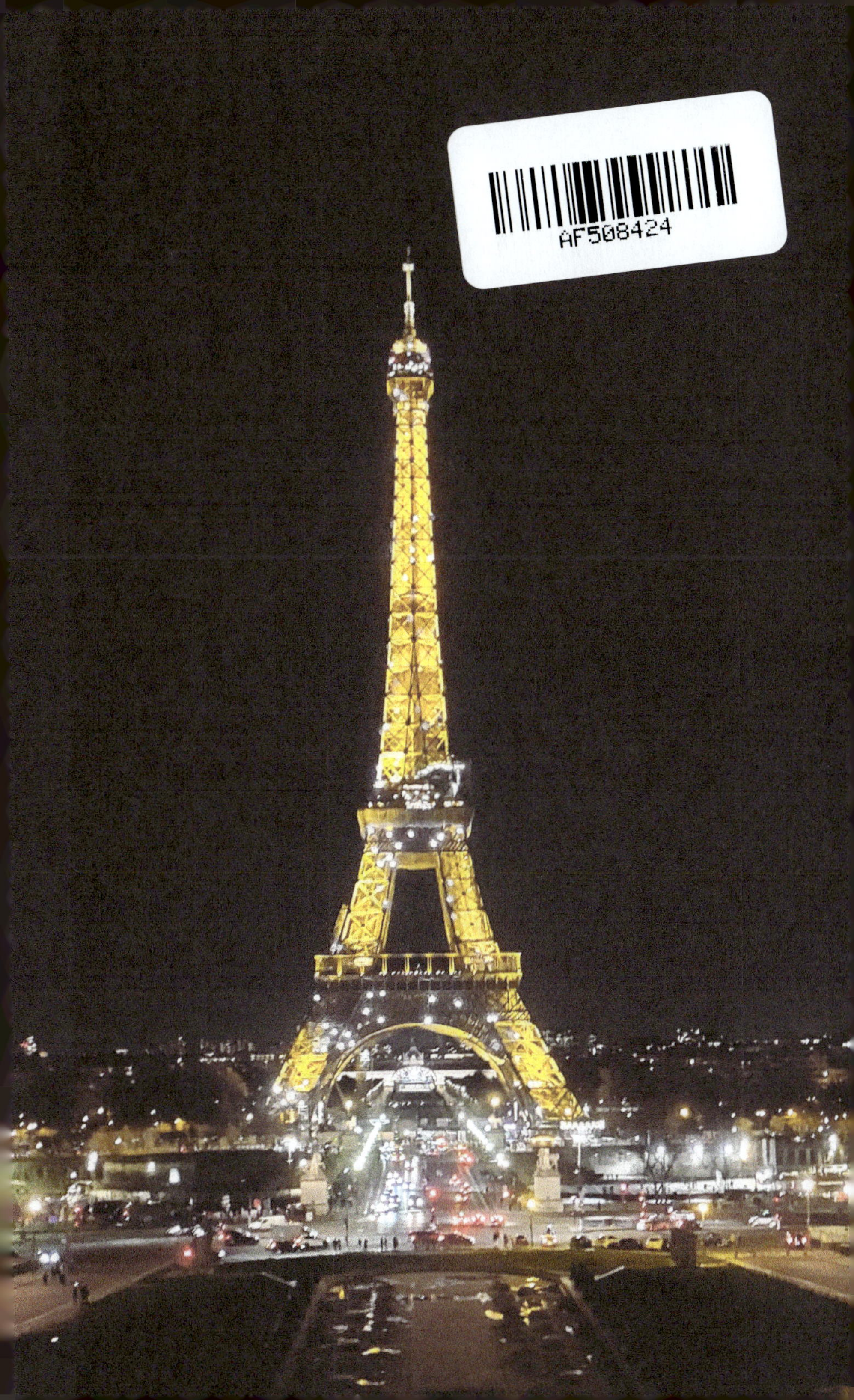
AF508424

PARIS FOR MUSEUM LOVERS

Paris for Museum Lovers

A 6-Day Journey for Art Lovers & Savvy Explorers

A.J. CAMPBELL

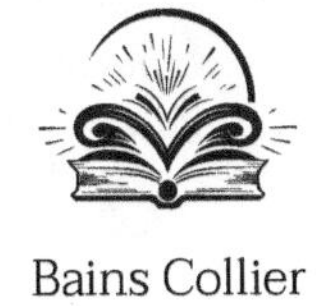

Bains Collier

To my wonderful family with whom I would travel the world.

Contents

Chapter 1

Paris

Do you want Parisian picture-perfect moments to share on Instagram? You know, the ones you see all over social media with people striking poses in front of famous landmarks. Well, if you're looking for tips on becoming an Instagram influencer, sorry, wrong guide! I can't help you get a reservation at Pink Mamma or discount tickets to the early show at the Moulin Rouge. But don't fret, my friend, because what I can offer you is much more.

Our journey begins with a simple truth: Paris is expensive. Planning and insider knowledge allow you to navigate this pricey city like a pro. Forget about those fancy hotels with grand lobbies and room service. I am all about budget-friendly options here. Consider staying in modest but cozy hotels. Posh is fine, but if you are traveling alone or with a family, location and room size should matter more than a Michelin two-star restaurant in the lobby.

On my family's recent trip to Paris, we spent about $1,500 per person on the hotel and airfare for our six-day trip out of our budget of €1957.84 per person. There was no

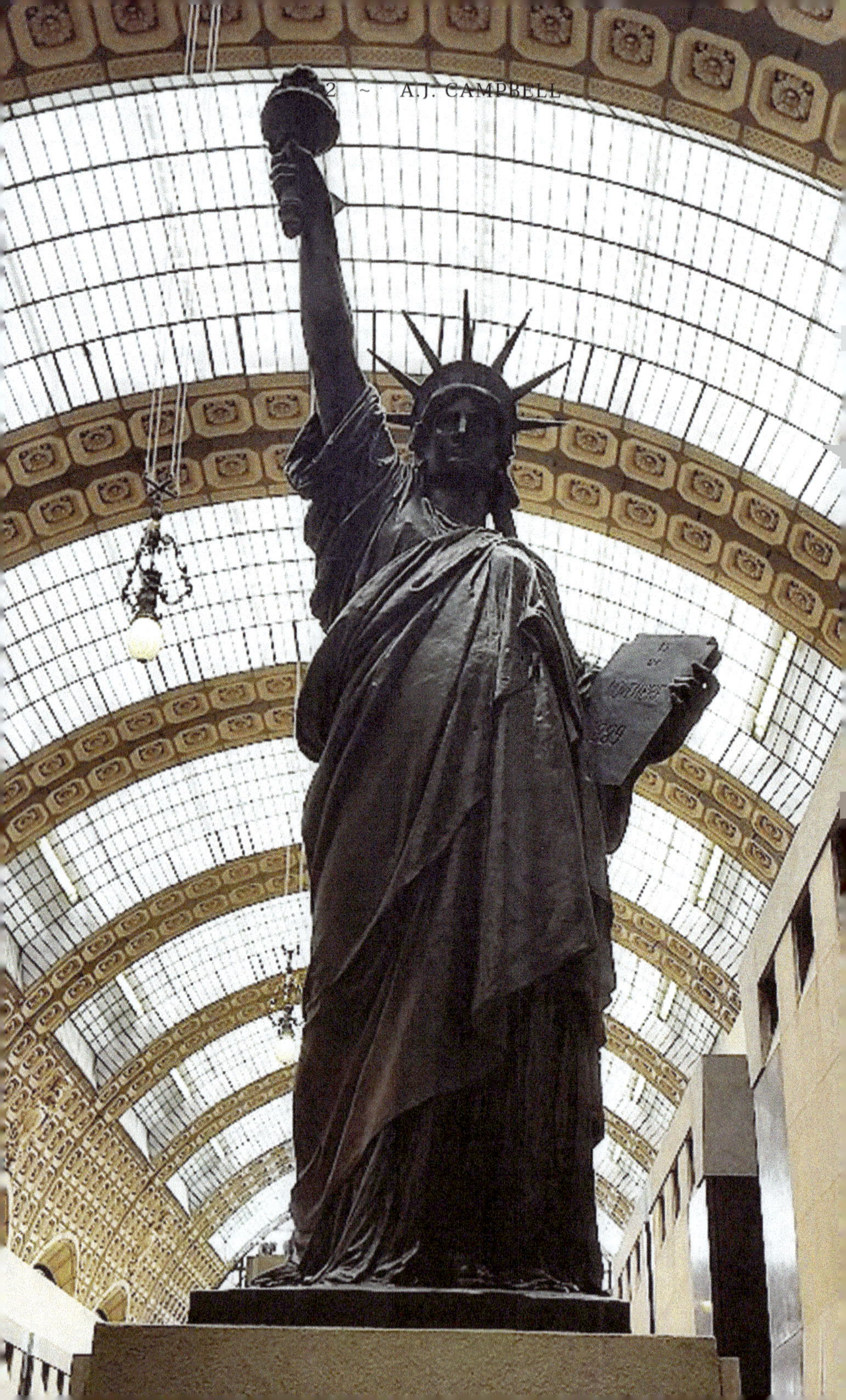

magic to it. I meticulously stalked the internet, messed with travel sites' marketing algorithms, and danced a hypnotic version of the Tarantella in the pale moonlight. I'm just kidding about a Tarantella, but all the rest is true. Travel is more expensive than it needs to be. More on that later, but your best bet is to go to the big travel sites and compare package deals on large airlines.

Traveling to Paris doesn't have to break the bank, but with my family, it usually does. I can confirm travel, entertainment, and food, but there is no way to budget for expensive splurge items. So, I don't even bother to try. Chanel handbags are not included in the budget. Side trips to the Vivienne Westwood boutique and museum giftshops were considered out-of-budget items.

That being said, experiencing Paris on a budget is feasible with careful planning and intelligent choices. Consider various expenses, including transportation, accommodation, food, entertainment, and unexpected costs. Look for budget-friendly accommodation options, explore local markets and street vendors for affordable dining, and take advantage of discounted admission to museums and attractions. Plan your itinerary around cost-saving opportunities and use the city's excellent public transportation system. By being mindful of your expenses and finding creative ways to save, you can enjoy the magic of Paris without compromising your budget.

Now, let's talk about meals. Ah, French cuisine is the epitome of culinary delight. But dining out in Paris can put a dent in your wallet faster than you can say "croissant". So, skip the expensive hotel breakfasts, head to the local boulangerie for a heavenly €1 croissant, grab a coffee, and take it back to your mid-priced tourist hotel. Now you have room service, and you get some exercise, too! Trust me, you won't be disappointed. For lunch, indulge in a baguette sandwich from a neighborhood boulangerie. Not only will it save you money, but it's also a delicious way to experience authentic French flavors. Take a sandwich and a water bottle with you to avoid long waits at touristy places at the museums. We brought sandwiches and ate them in the garden at Versailles. It was an excellent meal. I will never forget our golf cart picnic amongst the fountains and trees.

Here's where we go big! Dinner is our time to splash the cash. We've saved up by being thrifty during the day, so now it's time to treat ourselves. Find those local brasseries where you can savor delicious French standards with a glass of wine or a whole carafe. I have never had so much wine in my life. And get the desserts, please. Never skip dessert in Paris if you have room. Who needs a Michelin star when you can have a memorable culinary experience at a fraction of the price and eat like a local? Our food budget is $60 daily, almost all of that on dinner. If that is too steep, you can limit your dinners to smaller plates at brasseries with drinks, but try to have a posh dinner at least half the nights of your stay.

Now, let's dive into the heart of Paris—the museums. Oh, the Louvre, the Musée d'Orsay, Versailles—the list goes on. These cultural centers are a feast for the eyes and the soul. But don't worry; you don't need to spend all your Euros on entrance fees. We are savvy travelers and will use the Paris Museum Pass (parismuseumpass.fr) to save you cash. We got the four-day pass for €70.00. The four days are contiguous, so plan accordingly. Make sure the list of museums and attractions is what you want to go to and that nothing is missing. You only get to go to each venue once,

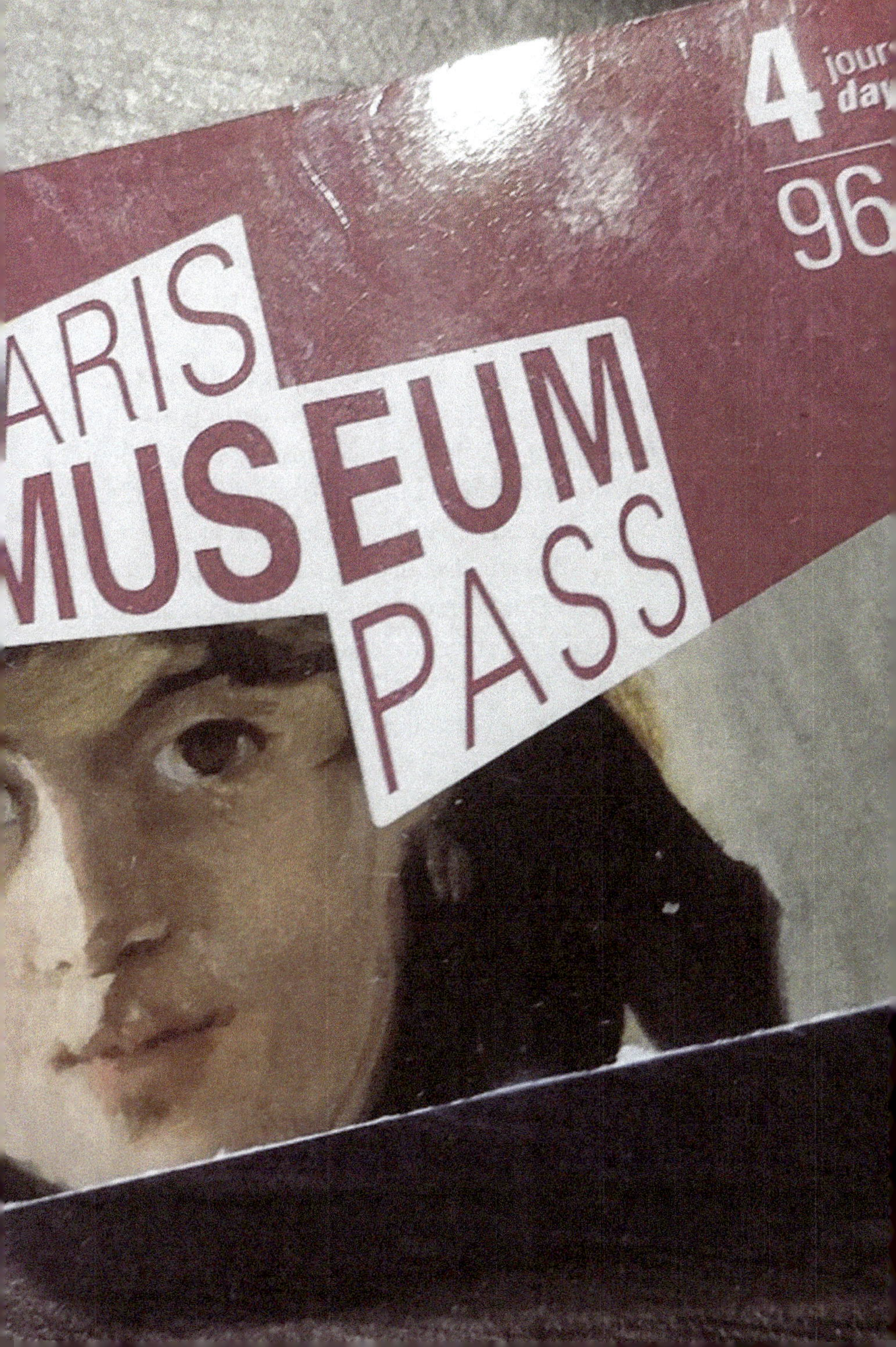

4 jour
day
96
ARIS
MUSEUM
PASS

and some places require advanced reservations, so go online weeks before you leave for the best time slots. For example, Versailles is a breeze when it first opens and is packed like a subway car in rush hour during the afternoons. Timing and reservations will make your trip easier and make your travel companions feel loved and cared for. Planning is my travel love language. I think of it as a gift to the people I love. Of course, my family calls it me being bossy, but I am working on this in therapy.

Getting around the city is another piece of the puzzle. Fortunately, Paris has an extensive and efficient public transportation system. Embrace the metro and busses and walk like a true Parisian, hopping from one neighborhood to another without spending a fortune on taxis. We will use a *Pass Navigo Découverte* card, or the Navigo Weekly Ticket (iledefrance-mobilites.fr/en/tickets-fares/detail/navigo-weekly-ticket) for cheap unlimited travel for only €30,75 to regions 1-5, which will get you all around Paris including Euro Disney, Versailles, and the airports. There are maps available and an app to download at iledefrance-mobilites.fr/en/the-network/maps-plans. Some restrictions have to do with the dates you arrive and leave, but if you are in Paris Monday through Sunday, you will receive the most significant benefit with the Navigo Weekly Ticket, which will pay for itself in a few trips.

Study the map, download the travel apps, bring a small photo of each person in your group, and enjoy the thrill of navigating the labyrinthine tunnels beneath the city. Some of the best views in Paris are on buses or the metro. Catch the Number 6 train for iconic over-the-Seine shots of the Eiffel Tower. Who needs a chauffeur when you can feel like a local on the metro?

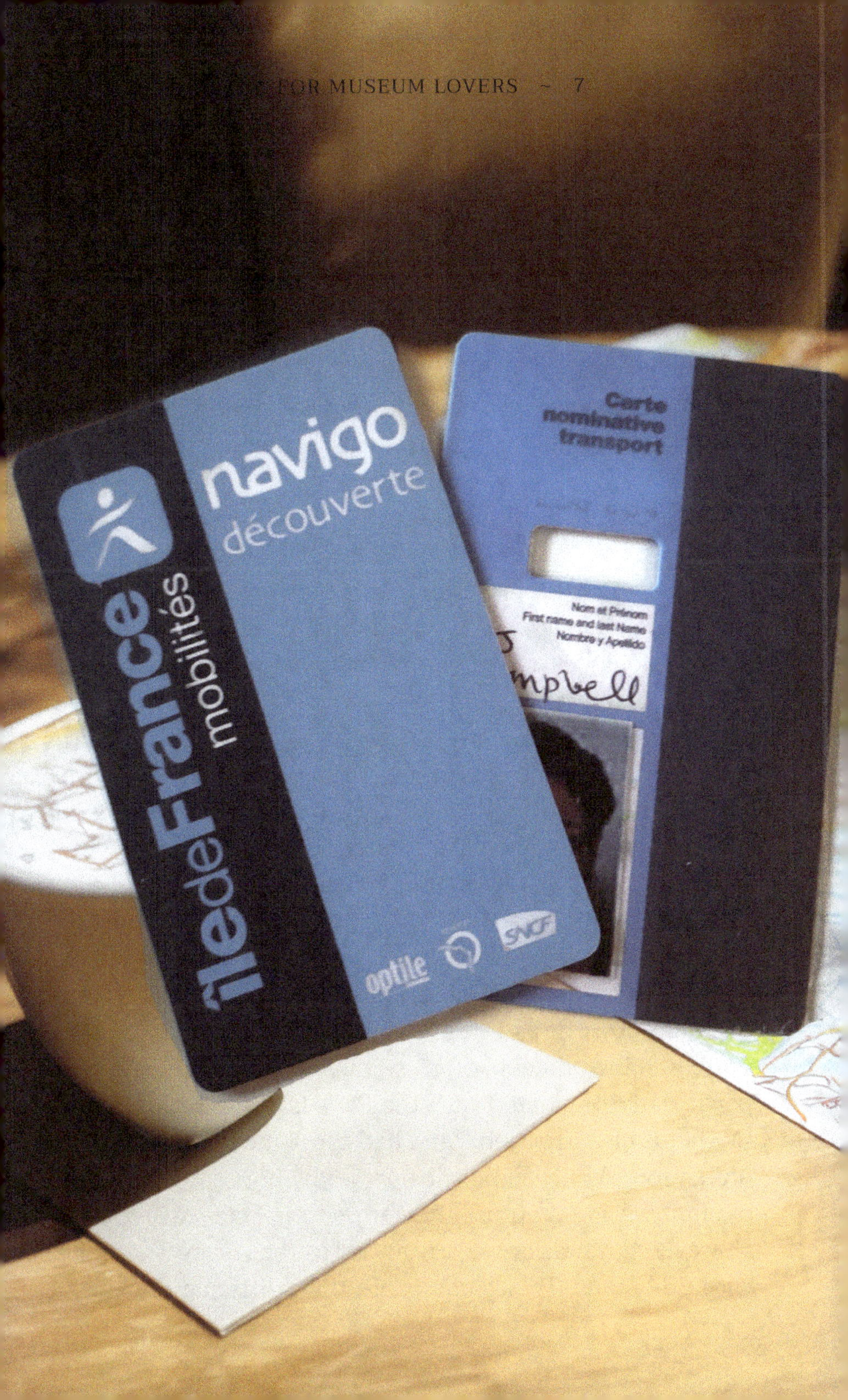
navigo
découverte
îledeFrance
mobilités
optile
SNCF
Carte
nominative
transport
Nom et Prénom
First name and last Name
Nombre y Apellido

So, my fellow Museum lovers, prepare for an unforgettable adventure through Paris. Say 'au revoir' to the overpriced tourist traps and 'bonjour' to the hidden gems and authentic experiences that will make your trip truly memorable. With some planning, a sense of adventure, and a willingness to stray from the beaten path, you can have a fantastic time in Paris without breaking the bank. So, go forth, explore, and make memories that will last a lifetime—all while keeping your wallet and your family happy.

The Itinerary Includes Everyone

Crafting the perfect itinerary for a trip to Paris requires careful consideration of your interests and travel companions' preferences and physical abilities. Everyone may have different expectations and desires, so it's essential to strike a balance that ensures everyone has a memorable experience. As a traveler, you must walk long distances, climb stairs, and stand for long periods. I am not an expert on accessibility travel, but if this concerns anyone in your party, you must study online guides like Sage Travel (sage-traveling.com) or the Wheelchair Travel Guide (wheelchair-travel.org/paris). Travel should be accessible to everyone, but it does take knowledge and planning.

I am not as fit as I would like, and many attractions require walking or steep, often spiral stairs. My daughter was particularly fascinated with the Paris Catacombs, while my mother is claustrophobic and had zero interest in venturing underground only to be surrounded by bones. I was scared of climbing 112 steps up the narrow spiral staircase to exit. However, that was not nearly as bad as the Arc de Triomphe with 284 steps. To accommodate their differing phobias, I scheduled a visit to the Catacombs in the afternoon, following a morning visit to the Musee d'Orsay. I took the stairs with the cocky enthusiasm of a weekend warrior, only to be flanked by septuagenarian German tourists urging me to go faster. It was like taking an underground, spooky step aerobics class.

Mom got the better part of the deal; I planned the Catacombs trip so my mom could have some time to explore Paris independently. She could return to the hotel for rest, go shopping, or relax at a nearby Parisian café. I knew that she would enjoy people-watching and immersing herself in the charming ambiance of the city. True to form, when we returned from the Catacombs, she had found a cozy corner café, sipping coffee and savoring a delicious bowl of onion soup while observing the lively Parisian scene. I half expected her to pick up her long-gone cigarette habit. To my surprise, she later revealed that it was the highlight of her trip. She appreciated the freedom to enjoy her time and cherished the authentic Parisian atmosphere she encountered during her café escapade.

Crafting an itinerary requires thoughtful consideration of your interests and travel companions' preferences. By creating a balanced schedule that incorporates various activities and allows for flexibility, you can ensure everyone has a fulfilling and enjoyable trip. Taking into account individual preferences and physical limitations and making necessary reservations in advance are all essential elements of a well-planned itinerary for a trip to Paris or any other destination.

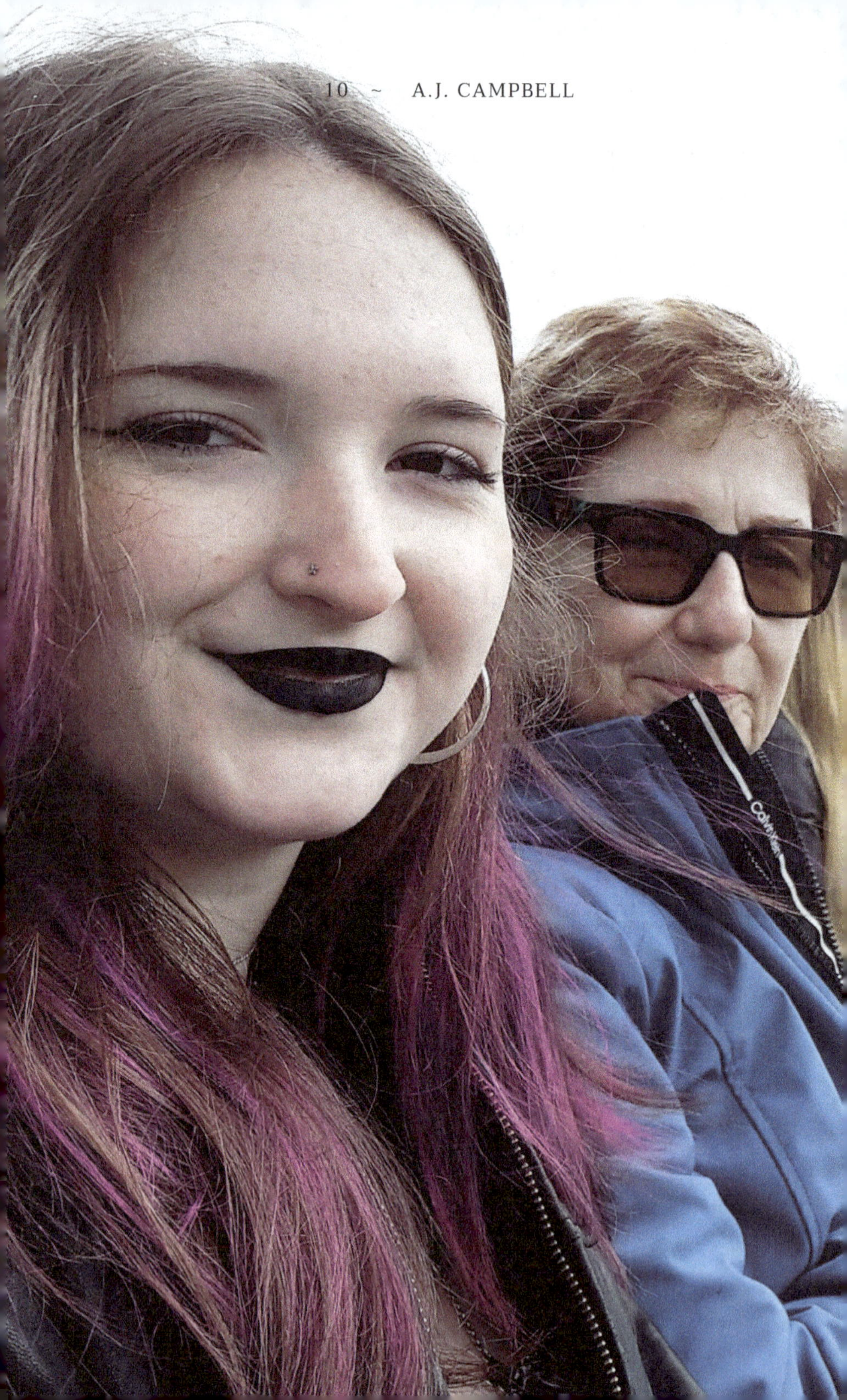

My Family's Baggage

I've lost count of how often I've tried convincing my family to pack light and leave behind unnecessary items. It seems like an impossible task. They cannot imagine traveling with a backpack or a small carry-on bag. For them, every occasion, every possible weather condition, and every potential scenario must be accounted for in their packing.

When we plan a trip, I meticulously research the weather, the local customs, and the activities we'll engage in. Armed with this knowledge, I carefully select a few versatile outfits that can be mixed and matched to suit any occasion. I emphasize the importance of packing lightweight and quick-drying fabrics that can be easily washed and dried on the go, but my suggestions fall on deaf ears.

Instead, my family insists on packing bulky sweaters and heavy jackets alongside summer swimsuits in the winter and an array of footwear suitable for any terrain, from sandals to snow boots for the same trip. It's not uncommon to see them dragging suitcases twice their size, struggling to fit them in taxi trunks, or maneuvering them through crowded airports. While they may be prepared for any weather condition or fashion emergency, the burden of their excessive packing weighs heavily on me. Not in a symbolic way - I always get stuck carrying their baggage.

During our trips, I often make last-minute adjustments to our plans. Sometimes, we stumble upon an exciting detour or extend our stay in a particular location. In such situations, flexibility is crucial, and traveling light allows for spontaneous changes without logistical nightmares. However, my family's insistence on overpacking means we must make additional arrangements like hiring car services to accommodate our excess baggage or paying hefty flight check-in fees.

I've tried reasoning with my family, explaining the benefits of traveling light: the freedom of movement, the convenience, and the financial savings. But it's an uphill battle. Their attachment to their belongings and the comfort of having everything at their disposal outweigh any logical argument I present. I have spent years talking about this to them, but it doesn't make any real difference. So, I have taught myself to roll with the roller bag. On this last trip, I brought an extra empty suitcase inside my luggage so that there was room for everything when the bags of clothes needed to make the flight back home.

Despite the challenges, I must remind myself that my family's baggage goes beyond physical belongings. It metaphorically represents their quirks, idiosyncrasies, and attachments. It's a part of who they are, and as frustrating as it can be at times, it's also what makes them the people I would rather spend time with than anyone on the planet.

So, I've learned to embrace the chaos and accept that our family vacations will always involve hauling heavy bags and maneuvering through crowded spaces. Ultimately, the shared experiences, the laughter, and the memories we create together ultimately matter the most. No matter how much we bicker about packing, I wouldn't trade them for the world.

Perhaps one day, they'll glimpse the freedom and ease of traveling light. Until then, I'll pack my minimalist backpack, hoping they'll eventually come around. And in the meantime, I'll be there to lend a helping hand whenever their overloaded suitcases become too burdensome to bear.

The Schedule

Once you have a well-crafted itinerary or have utilized the one provided, the next step in planning your trip to Paris is to schedule your days to optimize your time in the city. Paris is a bustling metropolis with many attractions, so careful time management ensures you make the most of your visit.

Start by breaking down your itinerary into manageable chunks by whole or half-days. This allows you to allocate specific activities and sightseeing spots to each time slot. Consider the proximity of the attractions to one another and group them accordingly to minimize travel time. Once you start, you will realize that some natural restrictions will come into play to set the first item on your schedule. For example, there are many closed days for museums. You might also check if your Museum Pass requires you to go to all your exhibits on back-to-back days or a certain number of days. Likewise, your travel pass will have day restrictions. Start with the most restricted items and work from there.

When scheduling your days, it's essential to consider the popularity of specific attractions and the potential for crowds. The Eiffel Tower, for example, is one of the most iconic landmarks in the world and tends to draw massive crowds. Plan your visit during off-peak hours to avoid long queues and ensure a more enjoyable experience. Early mornings or evenings are often less crowded, allowing you to appreciate the tower's beauty without feeling over-whelmed by the masses.

Additionally, factor in travel time when organizing your activities. Paris boasts an extensive public transportation system, including the metro, buses, and trains. While these options are convenient for getting around the city, it's essential to consider the time it takes to navigate the routes and transfer between different modes of transportation. Account for potential delays or unfamiliarity with the system, especially if you are new to Paris. Give yourself ample time to reach each destination, allowing for a buffer in case of any unforeseen circumstances.

I lost count of how often I missed the train or got turned around on the metro. We used a great app called City Mapper to navigate. I got the app to work on my phone and watch by some technological miracle. I got turn-by-turn directions and specific instructions on which part of the train to board and which exit to use. All that assistance, including my watch vibrating every prompt to turn, still got us lost sometimes. But we could recover and find the correct directions using the app. It would be best to consider many others from the transit authority, including Google Maps and Bonjour RATP.

By carefully planning your days and accounting for travel time, you can ensure a smooth and efficient exploration of Paris. Be mindful of the opening and closing hours of attractions and plan accordingly. Some museums and landmarks have specific time slots for guided tours or certain exhibits, so check their schedules in advance to make the most of your visit.

While having a well-structured itinerary is essential, allowing flexibility and downtime is equally important. Don't overpack your days to the point of exhaustion. Leave some room for spontaneous discoveries, strolls along the Seine, or savoring a cup of coffee at a quaint café. These moments of relaxation and uncertainty can often be the most memorable parts of your trip.

Consider your personal preferences and interests when scheduling your days. As an art lover, allocate more time for museum visits. If you enjoy culinary experiences, leave room for exploring local markets and indulging in French cuisine. Tailor your schedule to align with what resonates with you the most, creating a trip that reflects your unique interests and desires.

When planning this itinerary, I started with the underlying structure of the Navigo Weekly Ticket which has unlimited travel from Monday to Sunday. Next, I looked at the best dates and times to see the museums I wanted. Some were closed on Tuesdays or Mondays. It was essential to start there. After that, start filling in the days and stops you wish to see. It is an excellent place to start for your schedule or to modify my itinerary.

In conclusion, effectively scheduling your days in Paris is crucial for maximizing your time and experiencing the city. Break down your itinerary into manageable chunks, consider the popularity of attractions, account for travel time, and allow for flexibility. You can create a memorable and enjoyable trip that encompasses the rich cultural tapestry and enchanting ambiance by striking the right balance between structure and spontaneity.

Our Hotel Stay

Paris is a city known for its elegance, charm, and, unfortunately, being expensive. However, with careful planning and budgeting, it's possible to enjoy Paris's beauty and culture without breaking the bank. When

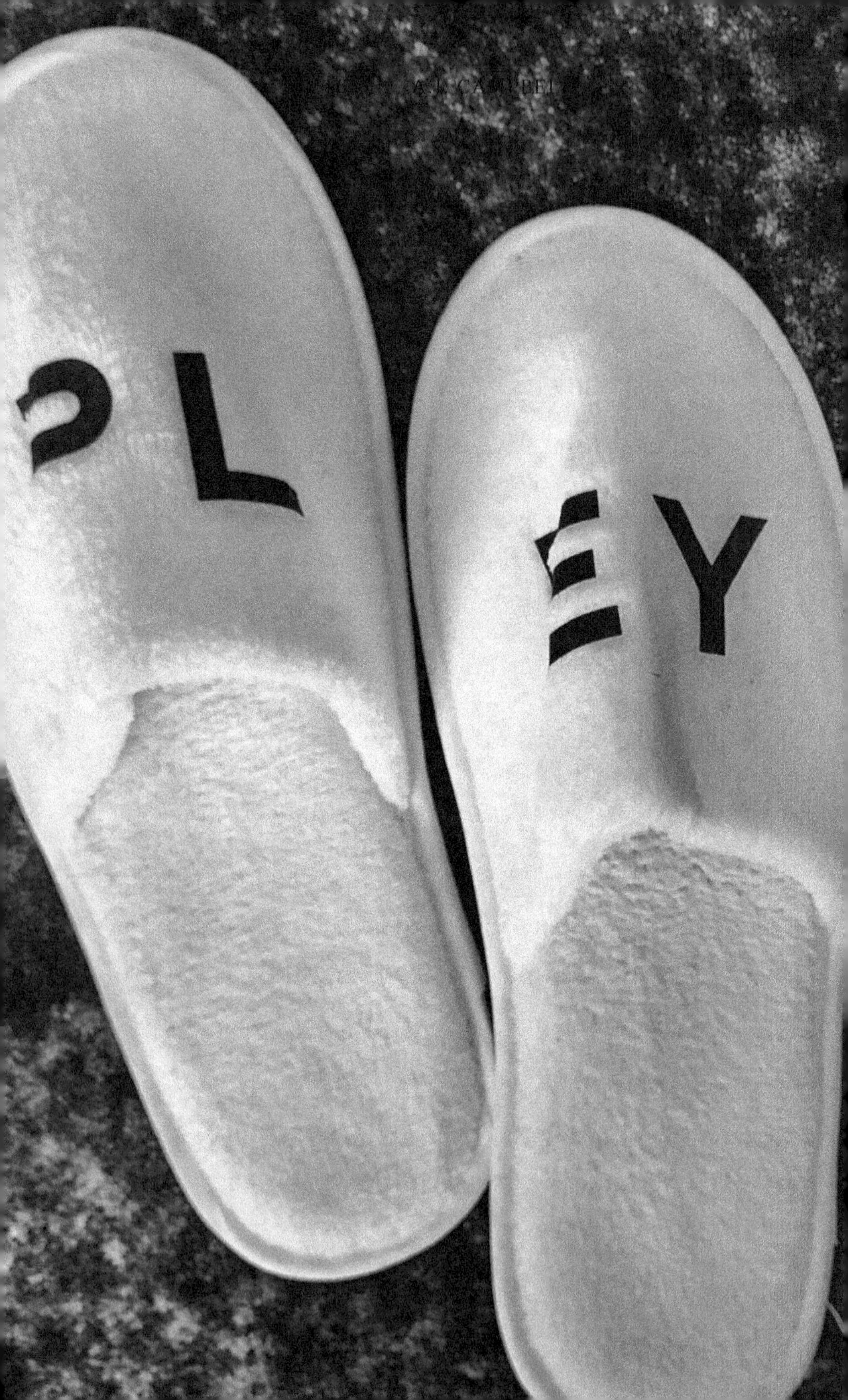

creating your budget for a trip to the City of Light, it's essential to consider various expenses, including travel, accommodation, food, entertainment, and unexpected costs.

Accommodation costs can vary significantly in Paris, but budget-friendly options are available. Consider staying in a budget hotel, hostel, or guesthouse, which can provide comfortable and convenient accommodations at a fraction of the cost of luxury hotels. Another popular option is to rent an apartment or a room through platforms like Airbnb, where you can often find affordable and well-located options. By opting for these alternatives, you can save significantly on accommodation expenses.

We stayed in the 8th Arrondissement, just a few blocks from the Arc de Triomphe and the Champs-Élysées. We wanted an accessible location with easy metro access to the one train that would take us to and from most of the attractions we wanted to see. We found, to our surprise, with a little investigation, that the 22 bus, which was right outside the hotel at the corner, took us to the Arc de Triomphe and the Trocadero, the best spot for photos of the Eiffel Tower.

I also considered the hotel we chose carefully in its proximity to a laundry mat, small grocery store, pharmacy, boulangerie, and brasseries. We wanted a place that would be easy to find things that we wanted or make our lives just a little bit easier. I also found a spa three streets away but never made it there.

Learning French

I have spent years working on my French skills since middle school. I had a particularly traumatic experience my in high school French class when the teacher told the entire class that I was not allowed to progress to third-year study because...well, I never really got a reason. My sincere desire to be able to speak French without effort has never paid off, no matter how many hours of Duolingo or Rosetta Stone I worked over the years.

I got to Paris, and waiting in line to go through customs was an eye-opener. I could not keep up with anything anybody was saying; I had trouble with word recall. It was like I was set back to high school French class all over again. But despite these early setbacks, I understood more than I spoke. Many shopkeepers and hotel workers spoke enough English to suffer from my low-grade French. When in doubt, I used my phone to translate, which worked out in the end.

Do not be afraid of not having a full grasp of French before going to Paris. The wonderful people of the city are used to dealing with the tourists who try in good faith. Start with a warm and welcoming "Bonjour", wait for them to say it back, then ask if they speak English, and gesture and point a lot. Most everyone has some words of English. When all else fails, use Google or Apple Live Translate. It is not perfect, but the Parisians will appreciate the effort.

What to Pack

Paris, the city of lights and romance, is a dream destination for many travelers. Whether visiting the Eiffel Tower, exploring the Louvre Museum, or strolling along the Seine River, there's plenty to see and do in this beautiful city. But before you embark on your Parisian adventure, planning and preparing for your trip is essential.

First and foremost, consider the weather when packing for your trip to Paris. The city experiences a temperate climate, with mild summers and chilly winters. Check the weather forecast for your travel dates and pack clothing appropriate for the season. In summer, lightweight and breathable fabrics, such as cotton and linen are ideal to stay calm and comfortable. Don't forget to bring a light jacket or sweater for cooler evenings. In winter, pack warm layers, including sweaters, coats, scarves, and gloves to protect yourself from the cold.

Your itinerary should also be taken into account when choosing what to pack. Paris has numerous cultural and historical attractions, including museums and churches. Some places have dress codes requiring visitors to dress modestly, with shoulders and knees covered. Pack clothing that adheres to these guidelines to ensure you can fully enjoy these sites. Lightweight cardigans, scarves, or shawls can help protect your shoulders if needed.

Comfortable walking shoes are a must when exploring Paris. The city is known for its charming streets and picturesque neighborhoods, perfect for leisurely walks. Opt for sturdy, comfortable shoes that allow you to navigate the cobblestone streets and sidewalks without discomfort. Pack a pair of sneakers or flats you can wear for long periods without experiencing foot pain.

In addition to clothing and footwear, consider bringing a small bag or backpack to carry your essentials while exploring the city. A bag with a secure closure will help keep your belongings safe from pickpockets. Having a map or a smartphone with navigation apps is always a good idea to help you find your way around Paris. Don't forget to carry some cash, as not all establishments accept credit cards, smaller shops or cafés in particular.

Please be careful when using the travel apps on your phone to keep it out of sight. Sadly, it is becoming more common that anyone would like to have phones snatched out of their hands. Many people have worn a lanyard or body chain to secure their phones. I kept my phone out of view by connecting it to my smartwatch. Your best bet is to keep your phone out of sight for as long as possible. You can also use an earpiece for turn-by-turn directions and keep your phone in your pocket.

In conclusion, consider the weather, itinerary, and local customs when preparing for your trip to Paris. Pack clothing suitable for the season and adhere to dress codes when visiting certain attractions. Don't forget comfortable walking shoes and a small bag to carry your essentials. Take advantage of the city's excellent public transportation system and familiarize yourself with the metro, buses, and other modes of transportation. By planning and being well-prepared, you'll be able to make the most of your time in the beautiful city of Paris.

The Arrondissement System

The arrondissement system in Paris has a fascinating history that dates back to the 19th century. It was introduced during the time of Napoleon Bonaparte as a way to organize and govern the rapidly growing city.

Before the arrondissement system was implemented, Paris had a complex layout and administrative structure. The city was divided into quarters, further divided into neighborhoods, making it difficult to establish a clear organizational hierarchy.

In 1795, a new law was passed to bring order and organization to the city. Under this law, Paris was partitioned into 12 arrondissements, each with a mayor and council. The arrondissements were designed to be roughly equal in size and population, with boundaries drawn in a circular pattern emanating from the city's center.

Over time, as the city grew, the number of arrondissements increased. In 1860, the city expanded its boundaries to include surrounding areas, and eight additional arrondissements were added, bringing the total to 20.

Each arrondissement in Paris has its distinct character and charm. We visited the first, second, and seventh arrondissements in particular. The first arrondissement, located in the city's heart, is home to iconic landmarks such as the Louvre Museum and the Tuileries Gardens. The second arrondissement is known for its bustling shopping streets and the historic Paris Bourse (stock exchange). The seventh arrondissement is where you'll find the Eiffel Tower and the majestic Invalides complex.

The arrondissement system serves as an administrative division of the city and influences the daily lives of Parisians. Each arrondissement has its town hall, police station, and local services. It's not uncommon for residents to feel a strong sense of pride and identity with their specific arrondissement, referring to themselves as "Parisians of the Xth" (X representing the number of their arrondissement).

For visitors to Paris, understanding the arrondissement system can be immensely helpful when planning their itinerary and getting around the city. The numbering system is designed to be intuitive, with lower numbers closer to the center and higher numbers on the outskirts. This makes locating attractions, restaurants, and accommodations more accessible based on their arrondissement.

Moreover, each arrondissement has its unique atmosphere and offerings. The diverse neighborhoods of Paris can vary significantly in terms of architecture, shops, restaurants, and cultural sites. Exploring different arrondissements allows visitors to experience the multifaceted nature of the city and discover hidden gems off the beaten path.

Whether you're wandering through the charming streets of Montmartre in the 18th arrondissement, enjoying the vibrant nightlife of the 11th arrondissement, or immersing yourself in the artistic atmosphere of the 6th arrondissement, each neighborhood offers a distinct Parisian experience.

The arrondissement system in Paris provides an organized and structured way to navigate the city. It has its roots in the early 19th century and has evolved to accommodate the growth and development of Paris. Understanding the arrondissements can enhance your visit to the City of Light, allowing you to discover the unique character of each neighborhood and make the most of your time in this captivating city.

Getting Around Paris

When using public transportation in Paris, it's essential to consider the various ticketing options available. As mentioned earlier, the Navigo Weekly Ticket is popular for frequent travelers. With this card, you have unlimited access to all modes of transport within the selected zones, including the metro, train, RER, tram, and bus. It provides convenience and cost savings, especially if you plan on using public transport extensively during your stay. The Navigo Weekly Ticket costs €30 for a week of unlimited travel, and you'll need to purchase the physical card for an additional €5.

There are other options if you will not use public transport that much in Paris or use it only for a few days.

You can access a customer service window at any metro or train station to obtain the Navigo card. It's advisable to bring a small passport-sized photo or have the option to take one at the station. However, getting your photo from home is often more cost-effective. Please take a picture against a white background using a smartphone or camera, ensuring it meets the dimensions of 25x30 mm (2.5x3 cm). Then, print the photo at a local pharmacy or print store. Once you have your Navigo card, you can load it at the ticket machines or customer service windows with the weekly pass.

While the metro and tram are popular choices for getting around Paris, buses also offer a convenient option, particularly if you want to experience the city at a more relaxed pace or explore specific areas that are not well-served by the metro. With over 350 bus routes in Paris, you can easily reach different neighborhoods and attractions. Buses operate from early morning until midnight, offering a reliable service throughout the day. Remember that bus travel times can be affected by traffic, so it's a good idea to plan your journey accordingly.

Lastly, the RER (Réseau Express Régional) is an extensive suburban rail network that connects Paris to its surrounding areas. It's helpful if you visit attractions outside the city center, such as the Palace of Versailles or Disneyland Paris.

The RER trains operate on different lines labeled with letters (A, B, C, D, and E) and are integrated into the public transportation system. They provide a quick and efficient means of transportation for longer distances, particularly when traveling between the city center and the suburbs.

Paris offers a comprehensive public transportation system that includes the metro, bus, tram, and RER. Each transport mode has advantages and can be used strategically depending on your destination and preferences. The Navigo Weekly Ticket provides an economical and convenient option for unlimited travel within the selected zones. Whether you choose the speed and efficiency of the metro, the scenic views from a bus, the accessibility of the tram, or the reach of the RER, Paris's public transportation system ensures that you can easily navigate the city and explore its many wonders.

Several transit apps, including Citymapper, Google Maps, and RATP, can help you navigate Paris's public transportation system. These apps provide real-time information on schedules, routes, and delays and can help you plan your journey more efficiently.

Beautiful Things to Do in Paris

No trip to Paris is complete without experiencing the city's iconic landmarks and attractions. Known as the City of Light, Paris offers a plethora of cultural and historical treasures that leave visitors in awe. Whether you're an art enthusiast, a history buff, or simply someone who appreciates the finer things in life, there is something for everyone in this enchanting city.

One of the first stops on any art lover's itinerary should be the Louvre, the largest museum in the world. Housing an impressive collection of over 38,000 artworks, including the famous *Mona Lisa*, the Louvre is a haven for art connoisseurs. From ancient Egyptian artifacts to Renaissance masterpieces, the museum showcases the breadth and depth of human creativity throughout the ages.

Visiting the Palace of Versailles is necessary for those interested in French history. Located just outside of Paris, this opulent palace is a testament to the grandeur of the French Baroque style. Once the residence of French kings and queens, the Palace of Versailles boasts stunning gardens, exquisite architecture, and lavish interiors that transport visitors back to a time of royal extravagance.

Stepping into the Jewish Quarter of Paris, visitors are greeted by a vibrant and historically rich neighborhood. Home to the Museum of the Art and History of Judaism, this area pays homage to the rich Jewish heritage of Paris. The museum showcases a wide range of Judaica, including religious artifacts, ceremonial objects, and artworks highlighting the Jewish community's contribution to the city's cultural fabric.

Dominating the western end of the Champs-Élysées, the Arc de Triomphe stands as a powerful symbol of French patriotism and resilience. Built to honor those who fought and died for France in the French Revolutionary and Napoleonic Wars, the monument offers a breathtaking panoramic view of the city from its observation deck. Visitors can climb the spiraling staircase to the top and witness the beauty of Paris unfolding before their eyes.

Art enthusiasts will also find solace in the Musée d'Orsay, a former railway station turned museum specializing in

Impressionist and Post-Impressionist art. Housing an extensive collection of works by renowned artists such as Monet, Renoir, and Van Gogh, the museum allows visitors to immerse themselves in the world of these revolutionary art movements.

The Paris Catacombs offer a unique and eerie experience for those seeking a different adventure. Beneath the city's bustling streets lies a vast underground labyrinth of tunnels and chambers filled with the bones of millions of Parisians. This macabre attraction is a haunting reminder of the city's past and provides a glimpse into its underground history.

A Seine River Cruise is highly recommended to relax and enjoy the city's beauty. Drifting along the gentle currents of the Seine, visitors can take in the picturesque scenery of Paris, passing by iconic landmarks such as Notre-Dame Cathedral, the Eiffel Tower, and the charming riverside boulevards. Whether during the day or illuminated by the city's lights at night, a river cruise offers a different perspective on the city's beauty.

The Trocadero Gardens are the perfect spot for a stunning view of the Eiffel Tower. Located across the Seine from the iconic monument, these gardens provide an ideal vantage point for capturing postcard-worthy photos. The vast green spaces are popular among locals and tourists alike for picnics, leisurely walks, and enjoying the breathtaking views of the Eiffel Tower in all its glory.

Aside from its cultural and historical attractions, Paris is renowned for its café culture and shopping scene. A stroll down the Champs-Élysées is a must for luxury shoppers, with high-end boutiques and flagship stores of famous fashion brands lining the avenue.

Leaving Family Members Behind

Leaving children behind while you go on vacation can be particularly challenging. Finding a reliable and trustworthy babysitter who can care for your little ones in your absence is essential. Start the search for a babysitter well in advance to ensure you have enough time to vet potential candidates thoroughly. Consider contacting friends, family members, or neighbors for recommendations or utilize reputable baby-sitting services that conduct background checks on their sitters.

When you find a suitable babysitter, take the time to introduce them to your children before your trip. This will help establish a rapport and build trust between the sitter and your kids. Provide the babysitter with a comprehensive list of emergency contacts, including your contact infor-mation, a backup contact, and the contact details of your children's doctor. It's also important to share any specific instructions or routines that need to be followed, such as bedtime routines, dietary restrictions, or allergies.

For those with furry family members, finding the right pet sitter is crucial to ensure their well-being while you're away. Like finding a babysitter, search for a pet sitter well ahead of your trip. Look for individuals or professional pet-sitting services that have experience and positive reviews. It's essential to schedule a meet-and-greet between your pet and the potential sitter to assess compatibility and ensure your pet feels comfortable around them.

Provide the pet sitter with detailed instructions regarding your pet's feeding schedule, exercise routine, medication, and any specific behavioral or health issues they should be aware of. Give them your veterinarian's contact information and authorization to seek medical care if necessary. Additionally, leave behind enough food, treats, and any supplies required to last the duration of your trip.

If you cannot find a suitable babysitter or pet sitter, consider asking a trusted family member or friend to step in. Grandparents, siblings, or close friends who are familiar with your children or pets may be willing to lend a helping hand. Ensure that they are well-informed about the needs and routines of your loved ones and provide them with the necessary contact information and instructions.

Sometimes, it may be necessary to consider alternative arrangements, such as enrolling your children in a summer camp or boarding your pets at a reputable kennel or cattery. Research and visit these facilities in advance to ensure they meet your standards of care. Check their policies, amenities, and reviews to gain confidence in their ability to provide a safe and comfortable environment for your loved ones.

No matter the arrangement you make, it's essential to maintain open lines of communication. Establish a regular check-in schedule with your babysitter or pet sitter to receive updates on your children or pets while you're away. This will provide peace of mind and allow you to address concerns or provide additional guidance.

Leaving family members behind while you go on vacation can be difficult. Still, with proper planning and communication, you can ensure their well-being and enjoy your trip with peace of mind. Remember to express gratitude to those who help care for your loved ones, whether they are a babysitter, pet sitter, family member, or friend, as their support allows you to enjoy your vacation knowing your family is in good hands.

Let's Get Started

Paris is a city full of history, culture, and beauty. Planning your trip carefully and navigating the city can help you make the most of your time and create unforgettable memories. Paris has something to offer everyone, from iconic landmarks to hidden gems. We hope this guide has provided helpful tips and inspiration for your trip to the City of Lights. Remember to pack appropriately, especially for the weather, and respect the local culture and customs.

Chapter 2

Some Assumptions

I am the planner in my family. I will spend weeks working out the perfect travel plans to maximize our fun and enjoyment while saving money. I will obsessively watch travel videos and learn to avoid scams and hacks. I will produce graphics and maps, learn the public transport system, and study the language. I will send everyone links, updates, and budgets. All of which will be ignored. My beautiful, fantastic family couldn't care less. Have I mentioned lately how much I love them?

You might ask why I do this for my family when it is clear that they don't care about it. But there would not be a satisfying answer that doesn't take years and years of therapy. It is probably something about control or growing up in chaos or some perfectionism. But this book is about travel and not needing a lifetime of treatment. I have always found the journey to be the best therapy imaginable, particularly when it is well managed by a structured but flexible schedule that allows each family member time to be together and apart.

Have breakfast together, then go your separate ways. Head out early and regroup at dinner to share photos and stories. Laugh over mistakes and share a carafe of red wine. My mom and daughter love shopping for clothes, makeup, and perfume. I get stuck holding the bags. It is not fun for me, so I have compensated by creating space for them to shop while I am off doing anything else.

One of this itinerary's fundamental principles focuses on what I care about. I see travel as part of a Grand Tour, a way to experience history and culture through art. On this trip with family that has never been to Paris, I want to visit famous museums like the Louvre or the Musée d'Orsay. These institutions are home to some of the world's most famous artworks, and they offer a unique opportunity to explore the history and culture of France.

Another important aspect of this itinerary is the emphasis on saving money on food where possible. Rather than splurging on expensive hotel breakfast buffets, with its questionably dated sausage swimming in grease and bread rolls with the tensile strength of carbon fiber, I encouraged travelers to buy croissants and pastries for breakfast and sandwiches at the boulangerie for lunch to go. This philosophy saves money on food and avoids awful tourist traps for breakfast and lunch. Sure, go to Angeline at the Louvre if you want to pay for a hot chocolate in the middle of summer and wait in line, but wouldn't it be better to eat a great sandwich in the atrium for just a few euros? You are not in Paris to be a statue waiting in line; you are there to see the art and learn about French culture. Later in the day, you can splurge on a dinner at a local brasserie or cafe, complete with a glass of delicious French wine.

Another way to save money is by using public transport to get around. Full disclosure: my overpacked family makes getting around challenging, and I have had to resort to private car service at several points in our travels. But we always default back to subways and buses. We love having an almost free bus tour of the city or above-ground subway. One of the best views of the Eiffel Tower and the Seine is from the sixth train heading back to the right bank. It is the one all the social media influencers do. The locals are all a little over it and will caution you not to take any pictures of them as it violates their privacy.

No itinerary is perfect, and travelers should be prepared for unexpected challenges or changes to their plans. However, by prioritizing museum visits, saving money on food, and using public transport, travelers can create a memorable and enjoyable trip to France without breaking the bank. Whether you're interested in art, food, or culture, this itinerary offers something for everyone, and it's a great way to experience all that France has to offer.

Assumptions

This itinerary assumes a six-day stay in Paris. We were arriving on Monday morning at Charles De Gaulle airport. We reserved one room that slept three with a private bathroom at a moderately-priced hotel. It was essential that we could store our luggage at the hotel, have access to a supermarket boulangerie within a few blocks, and have easy access to the main attractions. We stayed in the 8th arrondissement near the Champs-Élysées and the Arc de Triomphe. The hotel catered to English-speaking tourists, had modern bathrooms and elevators, and had a laundry service nearby so we could avoid pricy laundry service fees at the hotel, since I can't get over the idea of having something cleaned at the hotel for the price of two bottles of wine.

Chapter 3

The Budget

Staying in luxury hotels in Paris can be expensive, leaving travelers with limited budgets unable to explore the city fully. During our visit to Paris, we chose to stay at the Hotel Pley (pley-hotel.com) in the 8th arrondissement. One of the primary reasons for selecting this hotel was because it catered to English-speaking tourists. The staff was charming and eager to make our stay amazing. They also had wonderful videos on YouTube. Being able to see the hotel on the videos was crucial to making sure we knew that this was going to be of great value.

One of the most significant benefits of staying in a tourist-class hotel in Paris is its cost-effectiveness. Paris is a beautiful city, but it can be expensive to explore. Accommodation is one of the most expensive aspects of any trip, and opting for a more affordable accommodation option can free up your budget for other experiences. By selecting a tourist-class hotel, you can save considerable money, which can be spent on dining out, visiting museums, or shopping.

On arrival in Paris, we stored our bags at the Hotel Pley, then ran out to the city to find something to eat and go shopping. I was exhausted and asked the hotel to contact us when the room was ready. At some point, I had been up for 28 hours and could not go forward anymore. I had hoped to sleep on the plane, but that was not in the cards. I plopped down in the lobby with my family, who immediately slept in the comfy chairs.

I can't tell for sure, but I think it was a bad look for the hotel to have travelers sleeping in the lobby. After five minutes of snoring, we scored a free upgrade to a bigger room with a lovely view of the Eiffel Tower. A fact that thrilled my family to no end. We waited and watched it sparkle at the top of the hour each night before heading out to a posh brasserie dinner.

I don't miss the overpriced room service or the overdressed bellhops. I am not that kind of traveler. I want to stay in a nice, clean room but don't care about being catered to. I live a simple life and tend to travel the same way. If I want to be catered to or have a fancy gym, I buy a day pass to a city day spa or gym. I should say that the Hotel Pley has a workout room and offers yoga classes on the weekend. Nothing feels better than a good stretch after a long airplane flight or a long day of sightseeing.

In addition to the above, staying in a tourist-class hotel in Paris can be an excellent way to meet other travelers. These hotels tend to attract a diverse group of people from all over the world. Sharing common areas, such as lounges or cafes, allows you to interact with other travelers, share your experiences, and learn more about their cultures. During my stay at the Hotel Pley, I met travelers from various parts of the world, and it was an excellent way to network and make new friends. The hotel had an amazing coworking spot with big tables and comfy desk chairs. It was nice to mingle with other tourists and share tips about the cool sites they visited.

Finally, staying in a tourist-class hotel in Paris can help you explore the city on a budget. Many tourist-class hotels offer free or low-cost amenities such as breakfast or Wi-Fi. Additionally, some hotels may provide shuttle services or discounts on attractions, making exploring the city easier without breaking the bank. The Hotel Pley offered free Wi-Fi, which made it easy for me to stay connected with my loved ones back home.

Paris is a beautiful city that offers many unique experiences. However, these experiences can come at a high cost, especially when staying in luxury hotels. Opting for a tourist-class hotel can allow you to explore the city on a budget while immersing yourself in the local culture. From meeting other travelers to experiencing local cuisine and exploring the city like a local, there are many benefits to choosing a more affordable accommodation.

Let's get to the details of our budget. Hopefully, you will find inspiration in it for your own trip.

The Budget

Public transit to and from your home airport is €3.64 or $4 on the metro in my hometown of Washington, DC. Your cost will likely be higher, but my metro rail system gives $2 rides to the airport on the weekend. Full disclosure: we ended up driving to the airport and parking there because my family has baggage, lots of it.

Flight + Hotel: (Expedia) €1,423.13 or $1,566

Non-stop flight on United from the East Coast to Charles De Gaulle and a six-night stay in a lovely tourist-class hotel in the 8th arrondissement, five blocks from the Arc and the Champs.

Navigo Weekly Ticket: €30.74 + €5

You will buy the pass at the airport's customer service window at the airport train entrance. You must bring a small photograph for the pass and sign it at the counter. You will pay €30.74 for the entire week from Monday to Sunday. The card is €5 each.

Museums (Museum Pass 4 days): €70

A list of included venues and discounts is available at parismuseumpass.fr/t-en.

Golf Cart at Versailles: €13.33 per person

Get the golf cart at Versailles (1 hour, €38 plus tax for up to 4 people, three adults, one child). For more information regarding golf cart rentals, visit en.chateauversailles.fr/plan-your-visit/facilities/small-electric-vehicles.

Food: €60 per day per person, €360

- Breakfast: €2-3 per person, free coffee in the hotel room or lobby, croissants, and patisserie from a local bakery. Skip the prix fixe breakfast. It usually is very bad, and it is not a great idea to load up early in the day as you want to be free to try different foods throughout the day.

- Lunch: €7 per person, street food or sandwiches bought from the local bakery.
- Dinner: €50 per person, including two glasses of wine. We splurge on dinner at local brasseries.

River Tour of the Seine: €16

Discounts are often offered for online purchases.

Paris Catacombs: €29

Ticket information can be found at https://www.catacombes.paris.fr/en.

Gallerie Dior: €12

Ticket information can be found at https://www.galeriedior.com/en.

Total per person: €1,957.84 or $2,154.38

Chapter 4

Prêt-à-Porter

Watching someone pack should not be as fascinating to me as it is. I am a total sucker for a well-packed bag. I adore watching packing videos. It is part origami and part magic trick to me. I know they are trying to sell me luggage, packing cubes, or just doing it for likes and views, but I am enthralled. I long to find the perfect under-seat bag with an optional charging port for a cell phone.

I wanted to bound onto the airplane at the last minute, barely dodging the closing of the door, adventure movie-style, only to dash to my seat just in time for the safety demonstration. You don't have to board with the hoard if you don't need the overhead bin space. I travel like this all the time. One backpack is under the seat in front of me, but I have only managed this feat domestically.

My personal packing peculiarities aside, not everyone wants to be as light in the luggage as I am, or at least I aspire to be. Members of my family are max-packers, so I understand the impulse. If possible, and I know that it may not be, everyone should have a single bag and then pack a smaller bag or backpack inside that can be checked or carried on for items you buy.

If all else fails, you can consider sending items home if you go overboard. FedEx international saver can get a package to the east coast of the United States for only €93.99 for a 5 kg (11 lbs) box, sized 24" x 24" x 24". It is not a perfect solution but it might just come in handy if you plan on doing a multi-city stop and want to be unencumbered.

They sell dresses in Paris, don't they?

You and the family must be realistic about what you'll need during your trip. If a dashing stranger wants to take you to a glamorous ball, you can buy a dress in Paris. So don't bring a ball gown or a cocktail dress unless you know you will wear one.

The French prefer in their everyday dress to choose clothes of good quality that can be worn repeatedly just by changing scarves and accessories. Think simple and classic more than fashionable. The American version of fashion is different from what the French acknowledge. When in doubt, wear black or beige, add a scarf or broach, and bonus points will be awarded for vintage French items. Double bonus points for anything vintage Dior or Hermes.

The week you leave for Paris, check on the internet for Paris flea markets for that week. If you want amazing items, swing by the famous flea markets to look at glorious vintage items or designer finds. Be prepared not to get a bargain unless you have vintage buying experience and your French is flawless, but you will get something delightful and unique that you can say ever so casually that you picked up in a delightful flea market in Paris for next to nothing. We will know that it is not true that you overpaid for it, but it will be our secret.

If you are determined not to purchase anything at a flea market for full price, then when you find something you want to buy, do not show too much interest, inspect it for about three minutes, return it to the shelf or rack, and walk away. Make it seem as if you looked at it but decided against it. Keep browsing and walking slowly till it is out of view, Go on your phone and burn up some of your data plan to check the online price. If the price is within 20 percent, you should return and buy it. You may also try to haggle a bit if your French is good or you think Google Translate won't decide that you would prefer to pay triple and add a tip.

Check out TikTok creator Alicja (tiktok.com/@alicjakissaa) for the correct and updated listings. See if you can squeeze in a few flea markets before or after one of the museums or for lunch.

Smart Travel Tips: Managing Your Laundry Needs in Paris

I want to share a golden nugget of advice that often goes overlooked but can significantly enhance your travel experience in Paris: managing your laundry! Traveling is about exploring, creating memories, and immersing yourself in new cultures. But let's face it, it also involves practical challenges, including laundry management.

When booking your Parisian getaway, consider the proximity of laundry facilities to your hotel. This may seem minor, but it can save hassle and time. You can travel light and still have all the benefits if you commit to spending an hour or less doing laundry.

Many laundromats use a cashbox system mounted to the wall. You can pay for a specific machine number and then return to start your wash. It's user-friendly and a glimpse into everyday Parisian life. Many also sell soap there, or consider buying laundry sheets before you go.

Use Google Maps to locate the nearest laundromat to your hotel. It's a simple trick that can make your stay much more comfortable. You'll find that most laundromats have short cycles (sorta), and many even offer combination wash/dry machines.

A pro tip? Sure, it is a travel book, after all. Do your laundry once during your stay, preferably halfway through. This ensures you have a continuous cycle of fresh clothes without spending too much of your vacation in a laundromat.

Costs can vary a little between laundromats. Some places have websites, but most do not. You can find a business listing on Google Maps with photos of the inside of the shop posted by the owners and clients. The laundromats are small, and people do not hang out in them. Most will start their laundry and then seek a coffee or drink nearby.

The prices are usually clearly posted on the wall or front window. You can expect to pay around:

- M washing machine at €5.50/cycle
- XXL washing machine at €10.30/cycle
- L Dryer at €1.50/10 minutes
- Laundry detergent at €1.30/packet
- Softener at €1.30/each

You can see by the prices that it will be close to €9 per wash/dry, but it will save you a lot of hassle in the long run rather than overpacking or paying for valet cleaning at your hotel if it is even offered. It will be worth every single centime (penny). I have been known to rewash all my clothes before heading home because washed clothes are easier to pack. When I get home, it is just one less chore to have to do to reset the house before starting work again.

If you have to use a service, you can try the pick-up and drop-off services which can be found at pressandco.fr, wast.fr/Pricing, or decompressing.fr.

During my last trip to Paris, I stayed at a charming hotel in the 8th arrondissement. I found a quaint laundromat just around the corner. While I had planned on doing laundry there, I had packed so light that I didn't need to wash. My family brought enough clothes for an expedition to the North and South poles, back and forth twice, and they didn't do laundry, but I definitely will do so next time.

While laundry might not be the most glamorous aspect of traveling, embracing these practicalities can enrich your experience. It's all about balancing the excitement of travel with the comforts of home, even in the heart of Paris.

Get Packing

Think about the weather and the activities you'll be doing. If you follow this itinerary, it will consist mainly of traipsing into and out of museums. You will spend hours in museums on your feet most of that time. Your shoe selection will make or break your trip. Sometimes, I have been miserable on a trip because I bought the wrong shoes. Not to mention when I decided to wear overalls and Timberlands on an airplane and was subjected to "extra" screenings to get through security. I am not sure culturally, but I may still be engaged to an airport screener named Scholss from the airport in Zurich. But I may have been getting the signals wrong.

Paris is known for its unpredictable weather, so it's important to pack versatile, layered clothing. A lightweight raincoat or a small umbrella is also a must-have. I purchased three umbrellas for our trip to make sure that one of my beloved relatives didn't show up with a kind of parasol that required an extra suitcase.

When packing clothes, limit yourself to a few basic pieces that can be mixed and matched. Pack neutral colors such as black, white, and gray that can be paired with different accessories to create different outfits. Avoid bulky items like heavy jackets or sweaters and use lightweight fabrics like cotton or linen. Packing a scarf or two can also add a pop of color to your outfits while keeping you warm on chilly days.

Another way to save space is to pack items that serve multiple purposes. For example, a pair of comfortable walking shoes can also be used for a night out, even if you don't think they are stylish enough. They are not stylish enough for Paris. Don't try to match the relationship with fashion that French people have. It is a fool's folly meant to drive foreigners crazy and overspend on trendy clothing.

A backpack or a crossbody bag can be used as a carry-on during your flight and double as a day bag during your sightseeing adventures.

Toiletries can take up a lot of space in your luggage, so pack travel-sized products or decant your favorite items into smaller containers. Many hotels provide basic toiletries, so check with your accommodation to see what's available. Pack any medications you need and a small first aid kit with essentials such as bandaids and pain relievers.

When it comes to electronics, limit yourself to the essentials. A smartphone with a good camera can replace a bulky DSLR, and a portable charger can keep your devices up throughout the day. Make sure to bring the appropriate adapters for your electronics, as the voltage in Europe is different from other regions.

Finally, don't forget to leave some room in your luggage for souvenirs and gifts. Paris is known for its shopping, and you don't want to miss out on the opportunity to bring home some unique and memorable items.

Packing light for a sightseeing trip to Paris is all about being practical and strategic. Packaging versatile clothing, multi-purpose items and limiting your electronics and toiletries allows you to enjoy your trip without being weighed down by heavy luggage.

Packed Items

It is an ongoing fight in my house about what to pack and leave behind on a long trip. I am forever looking for the least amount of clothing to bring on a trip, and it seems as if my mother and daughter are trying to break some weight-lifting world record when it comes to packing items.

Unlike my family, I never back beauty care products for a trip. I don't use much at my age anyway, but I prefer being a no-fuss on holiday. Most photo apps will allow you to add a full face of makeup, so if you get a photo you are not happy with, you can add a full face of contour or makeup for your social media postings.

Frankly, I like experiencing the products in hotels and pharmacies in Paris. The hotel we stayed at had a whole range of nice products to try, so there was little need to buy or bring our own, but that did not stop my family from hauling half of CVS with us to Paris. Did I mention a pharmacy right at the corner from the hotel?

Clothing Packing list

Three bras, six pairs of underwear and socks (three dresses, two sport, one peds), one pair of jeans, one pair of black pants, one pair of leggings, one light sweater, one heavy sweater (if warranted), three shirts, one dress shirt/ blouse (knitwear is your friend), one blazer, one dress, a sun hat or wool hat, a scarf (silk or pashmina style), gloves (if warranted), shoes: one pair of sneakers, one pair of dress shoes, one pair of leather walking shoes. Small bag of toiletries. Other items: a small first aid kit, toothpaste/ toothbrush, hairbrush, razor, and diaper wipes. Purchase sunscreen in the country as carry-on rules tend to make it hard to bring such items, but you might be able to find sunscreen wipes or other items.

Top Tip: When checking in, you should ask if the airline would consider checking your bags for no additional fee at the bag drop. I would always suggest packing light and taking your baggage with you on the plane, but you can never tell what happens after your luggage is separated.

Top Tip: Consider getting luggage with a built-in air tag or adding an air tag to track its location. The FAA has allowed Airtags in luggage since 2022.

What to Wear Sightseeing

As a travel expert, I can tell you that what you wear when sightseeing can make a big difference in your overall experience. Being comfortable, practical, and safe when exploring a new city is important. Here are some tips on what to wear when sightseeing in Paris.

First and foremost, do not bring a bag or purse when sightseeing. Not only does it weigh you down, but it also makes you a target for pickpockets. Instead, opt for a fanny pack or a money belt to keep your valuables safe and easily accessible. These bags are worn around your waist and hidden under your clothing. You can keep your cash, passport, room key, phone, and cards in your fanny pack or money belt. If you must bring a purse, only put disposable items such as gloves, hats, and scarves.

In addition to a fanny pack or money belt, it's a good idea to connect your watch or phone to a cardless payment method through an app like Google Pay. Many places in Paris now only accept contactless payments, so having this set up in advance will make your transactions much smoother. This way, you won't have to worry about carrying cash or cards with you and can focus on enjoying your sightseeing.

Another important factor to consider when choosing what to wear sightseeing in Paris is comfort. When it comes to clothing, comfort should be your top priority. Paris is known for its cobblestone streets, so wear comfortable shoes that can handle a lot of walking. Avoid high heels or uncomfortable shoes as they only cause blisters and sore feet. Sneakers or walking shoes are a great choice for sightseeing.

Paris is a stylish city, but it's also a conservative one. Avoid wearing revealing clothing such as shorts, crop tops, or anything too tight. Instead, opt for comfortable clothing such as loose-fitting pants, mini skirts, or dresses that cover your knees.

When it comes to accessories, keep it simple. A scarf or hat can add color to your outfit and keep you warm on chilly days. Sunglasses are also a must-have for sunny days. Avoid wearing expensive jewelry or watches as they can attract unwanted attention.

What you wear when sightseeing in Paris can greatly impact your overall experience. Be practical, comfortable, and safe by avoiding bags or purses and opting for a fanny pack or money belt. Dress in layers, choose comfortable shoes, and opt for loose, comfortable clothing. Keep your accessories simple and avoid anything too flashy or expensive. By following these tips, you'll be able to enjoy your sightseeing adventure in Paris without issue.

Chapter 5

Getting Around Paris

The Paris transit system, known as the Régie Autonome des Transports Parisiens (RATP, ratp.fr/en), is one of the world's largest and most efficient public transportation systems. With a network of buses, trains, and metro lines, it serves millions of people daily, making it a crucial part of life for Parisians and visitors alike.

If you are staying in the city center, there is no better way to get around than the public transit system besides walking. Many Parisians prefer to walk great distances as part of their daily life, or some split the difference by taking the bus or train one way and walking back.

Because I am not as fit as an 80-year-old Parisian, I try to use a combination of walking and public transport wherever possible. It is good for the environment, saves money, and gives you a feel for the local life. It will be our primary mode of transportation around the city, getting us from the airport to the city and out to Versailles.

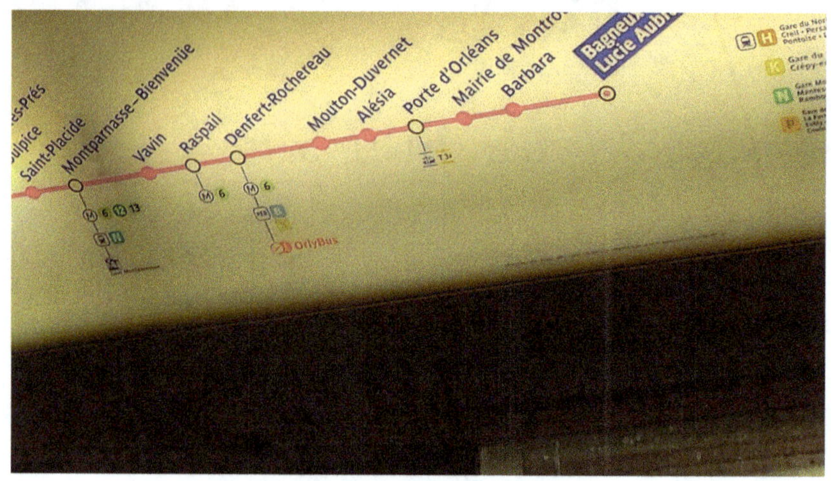

Paris metro Line 4 inside the car
by A. J. Campbell

Useful URLs for the Transit System

Navigo Découverte Travel Card
https://www.iledefrance-mobilites.fr/en/tickets-fares/media/navigo-decouverte-travel-card

Smartphone Tickets
https://www.iledefrance-mobilites.fr/en/tickets-fares/media/smartphone

The Île-de-France Mobilités network
https://www.iledefrance-mobilites.fr/en/the-network

History

The history of the Paris transit system is a fascinating journey through time, reflecting the city's evolution and technological advancements. Its origins can be traced back to the early 19th century, marking the beginning of a transportation revolution in one of the world's most iconic cities.

In 1828, Paris witnessed the introduction of the first horse-drawn omnibus line. This innovation marked a significant leap in urban transportation, offering Parisians a novel means of navigating the bustling city streets. The success of the omnibus paved the way for further advancements. By 1855, the transit landscape of Paris had undergone another major transformation with the construction of the first steam-powered train line between Paris and Versailles. This line connected Paris to its suburban areas and symbolized the dawn of a new era in mass transit.

The late 19th and early 20th centuries were a period of rapid growth and innovation. During this time, the city's transit system expanded to include electric trams and buses, revolutionizing public transportation with these cleaner and more efficient technologies. However, the most significant milestone was the inauguration of the first metro line in 1900. Coinciding with the Paris World's Fair, the opening of this line marked a pivotal moment in the city's history, laying the foundation for what would become one of the world's most extensive and renowned underground transit systems.

The role of the Paris transit system during World War II is a testament to its significance beyond mere transportation. During this period, the system played a crucial role in the resistance movement against the Nazi occupation. Many transit workers bravely engaged in sabotage and defiance, turning the network of trains and buses into a silent battleground of resistance. The metro tunnels and stations, often used as shelters during air raids, became symbols of resilience and hope amidst the darkness of war.

In the post-war era, the Paris transit system entered a phase of extensive modernization and expansion. Recognizing the need to accommodate the city's growing population and the increasing demand for efficient public transportation, several new metro lines and stations were constructed. This period saw the extension of existing lines and the addition of new ones, weaving an ever more complex web beneath the streets of Paris. Introducing newer, faster trains and expanding bus routes enhanced the system's capacity and reach.

Today, with its rich history, the Paris transit system is a living museum of urban transportation. Each line, station, and vehicle tells a story of technological progress, cultural shifts, and the unyielding spirit of a city that has long been at the forefront of innovation. From the horse-drawn omnibuses of the 19th century to the high-speed, automated metro trains of the 21st, the evolution of Paris's transit system mirrors the evolution of the city itself – constantly moving, adapting, and leading the way into the future.

Metro

The Paris metro, a marvel of urban transportation, is the backbone of the city's public transit system. Its extensive network comprised of 16 lines and over 300 stations serves millions of riders daily, weaving through the city's historic streets and modern neighborhoods. This system is not just a means of transportation; it's a symbol of Parisian culture and history, distinguished by its distinctive Art Nouveau architecture. Many stations are a testament to artistic and architectural ingenuity, featuring ornate tilework, elegant wrought-iron railings, and other decorative elements that transform mundane commutes into an aesthetic experience.

Operating hours for the metro stretch from around 5:30 am to 1:15 am, catering to early birds and night owls alike. During peak hours, trains arrive every 2-3 minutes, a testament to the system's efficiency and commitment to meeting the high demand of a bustling metropolis. In off-peak hours, the frequency adjusts to every 5-10 minutes, ensuring consistent daily service.

The fare structure of the Paris metro is designed with simplicity and accessibility in mind. The city is divided into five zones, with fares calculated based on the distance from the city center. A single ride within zones 1-2 is priced at €1.90, offering an affordable option for short trips. A 10-ride pass at €16.90 presents a cost-effective solution for frequent travelers. Additionally, we have opted for the Navigo Weekly Discovery card which offers unlimited travel within the specified zones, providing us with the flexibility and freedom to explore Paris at our leisure.

One of the most intriguing aspects of the Paris metro is the presence of unmanned trains on certain lines. For those accustomed to trains with conductors, this might initially seem disconcerting. However, these automated trains are a marvel of modern technology, offering a smooth and consistent ride akin to the trams found in many international airports. The seamless operation of these unmanned trains is a testament to the advanced infrastructure and commitment to innovation in Parisian public transport.

Riding the Paris metro is more than just a practical way to navigate the city. It's an immersive experience that offers a glimpse into the daily life of Parisians. Each journey is an opportunity to observe the diverse tapestry of Paris's neighborhoods, from the historic charm of Le Marais to the bustling streets of Montparnasse. The metro stations are like subterranean galleries, each with a unique character and story, reflecting the city's rich history and artistic heritage.

The Paris metro is vital to the city's vibrant life, providing an efficient, reliable, and uniquely charming way to explore the City of Lights. Whether it's a daily commute or a journey to discover the hidden gems of Paris, the metro is an indispensable tool for navigating this enchanting city.

Bus

The Paris bus system, integral to the city's extensive public transit network, boasts a remarkable expanse of over 350 routes. This intricate web of routes is serviced by thousands of buses, catering to the daily transportation needs of millions of riders. The buses commence their daily operations around 5:30 am, continuing until midnight. Notably, certain routes extend their service well into the night, accommodating the varied schedules of Parisians and tourists alike.

The fare structure of the Paris bus system mirrors that of the metro, employing a zone-based system. This approach ensures a seamless and integrated experience for commuters, as the same rates and pass options apply across different modes of public transport. This uniformity in pricing and accessibility is particularly beneficial for tourists and locals who rely on multiple forms of transit for their daily commute.

Some offer a distinctly picturesque journey through the city among the myriad of routes. A prime example is the

"Montmartrobus" route, renowned for its scenic meander through the enchanting streets of Montmartre. This route, among others, provides a unique vantage point from which to absorb the city's charm, far removed from the underground confines of the metro.

Our initial hesitation to utilize the bus system was soon overcome by the realization of its convenience and efficiency. As tourists, our primary goal was to optimize our time, balancing the desire to immerse ourselves in the rich cultural tapestry of Parisian museums with the simple pleasures of a leisurely, extended lunch in a quaint café. The bus system proved invaluable, facilitating swift and reliable transit across the city.

One night, the transit slowed down, and we had to wait a long time for a very crowded bus. Mom barely made it on, and there was no room for anyone else. The bus doors shut closed and took off. My daughter and I were left at the curb. We arranged to meet for dinner at the brasserie around the corner from the hotel. So my daughter and I set back on foot. We made it there before the bus due to the slowdown and overcrowding. My mother still says the overcrowding on the bus and her absence of a suitable mask is how she contracted COVID-19. We may never know, but I would not doubt it.

The significance of the bus system was further underscored when we had to adhere to strict schedules, such as timed entries to museums or boat cruises. The punctuality and extensive coverage of the bus routes ensured that we could reach our destinations promptly, thus avoiding the disappointment of missing out on pre-booked experiences. This aspect of the bus system was particularly appreciated, as it alleviated the stress associated with time-sensitive plans.

Moreover, the bus rides became an unexpected highlight of our Parisian adventure. Each journey offered a window into the city's daily life, presenting an ever-changing tapestry of neighborhoods, from the opulent avenues of the Champs-Élysées to the bohemian alleys of the Latin Quarter. We found ourselves captivated by the sights and sounds that unfolded before us, each bus ride contributing to a richer understanding and appreciation of Paris.

The Paris bus system is not merely a means of transportation; it is a gateway to the city's heart, offering a blend of efficiency, accessibility, and cultural immersion. For any visitor to Paris, venturing onto the bus is not just a practical choice but an opportunity to experience the city in all its multifaceted glory.

RER

The RER, or the Réseau Express Régional, is a cornerstone of Paris's public transportation network, offering a seamless blend of urban and suburban connectivity. This regional train network, encompassing five distinct lines, is ingeniously integrated into the fabric of Paris and its sprawling suburbs. The RER's design and operation are a testament to the city's commitment to efficient, comprehensive transit solutions.

Each line of the RER has been strategically laid out to serve key areas of the city and its outskirts. Its stations are underground, particularly in the city center, where they dovetail with Paris's architectural and historical landscape. This subterranean feature preserves the aesthetic integrity of the city's streetscapes and facilitates easy access to various neighborhoods and landmarks.

A significant advantage of the RER is its integration with the Paris metro system. Passengers can effortlessly transfer between the RER and Metro lines at numerous points throughout the city. This interconnectedness is a boon for commuters and tourists alike, enabling them to navigate the city and its environs with remarkable ease and efficiency.

Fare structuring for the RER is consistent with that of the Metro and bus systems, employing a zone-based system. For travel within zones 1-2, a single RER ride is priced at €2.90, while a 10-ride pass is available for €25.90, catering to occasional and frequent travelers.

Our Navigo card, a popular choice among residents and visitors, offers greater flexibility and value. With this card, one can travel unlimitedly within zones 1-5 on the RER and on the Metro and bus networks without incurring additional charges. The Navigo card's convenience is evident in its simple operation: passengers merely need to use their card at the entry and exit gates to access the RER network. This ease of use, combined with the comprehensive coverage of the card, makes it an ideal option for those looking to explore Paris and its surrounding areas extensively.

The RER is more than just a regional train network; it is a vital component of Paris's public transit ecosystem, bridging the gap between the city's heart and its suburbs. Its integration with other transit systems and flexible fare options like the Navigo card ensures that the RER remains an indispensable tool for efficient and accessible travel in and around the City of Lights.

Tram

The Paris tram system, a relatively recent addition to the city's extensive public transit network, has quickly become vital to the transportation landscape. With its expanding network of lines and stations, the tram system primarily serves the outer suburbs, connecting areas that are less accessible by metro or bus. This network, known as the Île-de-France tramways (French: Tramways d'Île-de-France), has grown to encompass thirteen operational lines, with more under construction and planning stages, showcasing the city's commitment to comprehensive and sustainable mobility solutions.

While predominantly serving suburban regions, the tram lines also have a significant presence within the limits of Paris. Lines T3a and T3b operate entirely within Paris, while lines T2 and T9 commence their routes within the city's borders. This integration ensures the tram system caters to commuters and tourists who wish to explore beyond the traditional city center. Many tram routes pass through scenic areas and charming neighborhoods, offering a pleasant and picturesque journey.

Fare structuring for the tram system aligns with that of the metro, busses, and RER, maintaining consistency across Paris's public transportation network. This uniformity in pricing and the availability of various pass options simplify the travel experience for both residents and visitors, allowing easy access to different zones across the city and its suburbs.

Though each line operates independently, the tram network is designed to be interconnected. Strategic connections exist between several lines, such as between T2 and

T3a at Porte de Versailles since 2009 and between T3a and T3b at Porte de Vincennes since 2012. These connections facilitate seamless transfers and enhance the network's efficiency. Once fully realized, the overall design of the tram network aims to be highly integrated, providing comprehensive coverage and convenient transit options across the Île-de-France region.

Most tram lines are operated by the Régie Autonome des Transports Parisiens (RATP), which manages the Paris Métro and most bus services in the immediate Paris area. This ensures a high standard of service and operational consistency across different modes of transport. Interestingly, while most lines use conventional steel-wheel rolling stock, lines T5 and T6 feature rubber-tired trams, a unique aspect that distinguishes them within the network.

Lines T4, T11 Express, and T13 Express are notable for being tram trains, a hybrid of tram and train systems. These lines share tracks with main-line railways and are operated by the French national rail operator SNCF as part of its Transilien regional rail network. Line T11 Express, in particular, is operated by SNCF's subsidiary Transkeo. This innovative approach allows for greater flexibility and integration between urban and suburban transit systems.

The Île-de-France tramways represent a dynamic and evolving aspect of Paris's public transportation system. With its blend of urban and suburban reach, integration with other transit modes, and innovative use of technology, the tram system plays a crucial role in shaping the mobility landscape of the Paris region, offering a reliable, enjoyable, and efficient way for residents and visitors to navigate the city and its surroundings.

Transit Apps

Several apps can help navigate Paris. Here are some of the best ones:

1. Citymapper: Citymapper is an excellent public transportation app for getting around Paris. It provides real-time information on bus, metro, and train schedules and bike-sharing options. It also offers step-by-step directions and estimated travel times.
2. Google Maps: Google Maps is a popular app for navigating cities, including Paris. It offers detailed maps of the city and turn-by-turn directions for walking, driving, and public transportation. It also includes information on nearby restaurants, shops, and attractions.
3. Uber: Uber is a popular ride-sharing app that can be useful for getting around Paris. It allows you to easily hail a car and pay for your ride through the app. Uber is particularly useful if you need to get to a destination that is not easily accessible by public transportation.
4. Velib: Velib is a bike-sharing app that allows you to rent a bike for short periods of time. It is a convenient and affordable way to get around Paris, especially if you want to explore the city leisurely.
5. Paris metro Map and Route Planner: This app provides a comprehensive map of the Paris metro system and information on train schedules and directions. It also includes a route planner that can help you find the fastest and most convenient route to your destination.

6. The Paris Pass App: If you plan to visit several museums and attractions in Paris, the Paris Pass app can be helpful. It provides information on the various museums and attractions of the Paris Pass and a map and directions to each location.
7. TripAdvisor: TripAdvisor is a popular travel app that can help navigate Paris. It includes reviews and ratings of restaurants, hotels, and attractions, as well as maps and directions to each location.

Many apps can help navigate Paris, depending on your specific needs and preferences. Whether you are looking for real-time transportation information, directions to local attractions, or recommendations for restaurants and hotels, there is an app that can help you make the most of your visit to Paris.

Chapter 6

Cracking the Code: Outsmarting Travel Algorithms

In the digital age, planning a trip no longer involves just a map, guidebook, or trip to the travel agent. The rise of on-line travel sites has revolutionized how we explore and book our journeys. At the heart of these platforms are sophisticated algorithms, a blend of data science and marketing wizardry, working tirelessly to deliver personalized travel options. But how exactly do these algorithms function?

It's either magic or an elaborate scam, or maybe just a little bit of both.

The Core Function: Matching Demand with Supply

At the heart of every travel site's algorithm lies a fundamental objective: efficiently matching user demand with the available supply to get you to spend money. A seemingly straightforward task is a complex dance of data analysis and real-time decision-making involving multiple layers of information processing.

Efficiency can be read in many different ways, but it usually means maximizing profits for the business and less about getting you the lowest available prices. Just go onto sites like Hopper or Kayak and see the algorithm showing an array of prices for your exact trip based solely on what site you book through. The dance has become even more frenetic with the introduction of Ai to the rhythm section.

Ai is being used to forecast travel demand and supply more accurately and predict trends. It is only going to get more difficult to get travel deals. Just know that you might not be shown all available travel deals, it will depend on many factors, including the size of your traveling party and schedule.

Does this all work together to get you the best deal? Sometimes yes, sometimes no. To beat an Ai, you need an Ai that works against it. If adventurous, try OpenAi's Chat GPT with the travel plugin installed. It is a game changer for travel booking.

It still sounds like a scam. How does it work?

Data Aggregation and Integration: The first step in this process is aggregating vast amounts of data from diverse sources. This includes flight schedules, hotel room availability, car rental inventories, and details about local attractions. These data points come from various suppliers - airlines, hotel chains, car rental companies, and tour operators, each with their own databases and inventory management systems. The algorithm must integrate this disparate data into a cohesive, searchable format, ensuring that the information is up-to-date and accurate.

Understanding User Demand: The algorithm must first understand what the users want to match this supply with demand. This involves analyzing search queries, ranging from specific (e.g., a hotel room in Paris for a particular weekend) to broad (e.g., vacation ideas in Europe). Advanced algorithms go beyond just parsing the search terms; they analyze user behavior on the site, previous bookings, and even inferred preferences based on similar user profiles.

Real-Time Processing: The dynamic nature of travel services adds another layer of complexity. Flight seats get booked, hotel rooms are reserved, and car rental availability changes constantly. The algorithm must process this data in real time, ensuring that the options presented to the user are available and bookable at that moment. This real-time processing is crucial in maintaining the reliability and trustworthiness of the travel site.

Balancing Multiple Factors: When presenting options to the user, the algorithm balances several factors. Availability is a primary concern, but pricing is equally crucial. The algorithm considers the current market rates, special deals, and even dynamic pricing models where prices fluctuate based on demand and supply. Location is another critical factor, especially for accommodations and local attractions. User preferences, gleaned from past interactions and current search parameters, also significantly tailor the results.

Optimizing for User and Supplier Needs: These algorithms aim to find a sweet spot that satisfies both the user's requirements and the supplier's objectives. For users, this means finding the best match for their travel needs at a competitive price. For suppliers, it involves maximizing their visibility and sales opportunities. The algorithm must navigate these sometimes competing interests to provide a harmonious outcome that benefits all parties involved.

The core function of travel site algorithms in matching demand with supply is a sophisticated process that requires real-time data integration, understanding user preferences, balancing multiple factors, and optimizing user and supplier needs. This intricate process makes online travel booking a convenient and efficient experience for millions of users worldwide, but it may not give you all the available options. It may only give you the options that it wants you to see.

Personalization: Personalization is where these algorithms truly shine. By analyzing your past searches, bookings, and interactions with the site, algorithms can predict what kind of accommodation, flight, or travel package might appeal to you. This is achieved through a complex process called machine learning, where the algorithm continuously learns from the data it receives, becoming more accurate in its predictions over time.

Dynamic Pricing: One of the most intriguing aspects of travel site algorithms is dynamic pricing. This is where the price of a flight, hotel room, or rental car can change in real time based on various factors. The algorithm considers demand (how many people are looking at a particular flight), time (how close the travel date is), and external factors like weather conditions or local events. This dynamic pricing model ensures that the service provider and the consumer get a fair deal based on current market conditions.

Search Ranking: When you enter a search query on a travel site, the algorithm decides which options to display first. This ranking is influenced by many factors, including price, user preferences, platform commission rates, and service provider quality. The goal is to provide a list that balances what the user is looking for with what the travel service providers want to promote.

User Experience Optimization: Travel site algorithms also focus on optimizing the user experience. They track how users interact with the site, identifying patterns that lead to successful bookings. By understanding these patterns, the algorithm can adjust the site layout, recommend additional services (like car rentals or travel insurance), and even send targeted email reminders or offers designed to enhance the booking experience and increase the likelihood of a transaction.

This is exhausting already. How do I beat this and get the best deal?

- **Use Incognito or Private Browsing Mode:** When you search for flights or hotels, do it in incognito or private browsing mode. Travel sites often track your searches via cookies and may raise prices based on your repeated interest in a specific route or hotel. Incognito mode helps prevent this by not storing your search history.

- **Clear Your Cookies and Browser History**: Regularly clear your cookies and browser history if you're not using incognito mode. This can help reset any data the travel sites have collected on your search preferences, potentially leading to lower prices.

- **Be Flexible with Your Travel Dates**: Prices can vary significantly based on the time of year, day of the week, and even time of day. If you have flexibility, try searching for different dates to see if prices are lower. Some travel sites offer a calendar view that shows how fares change on different days.

- **Book Well in Advance or Last Minute**: Booking either well in advance or at the last minute can sometimes yield better deals. Airlines and hotels are looking to fill seats and rooms. However, this strategy can be a bit of a gamble, especially if you have specific dates and locations in mind.

- **Compare Prices Across Multiple Sites**: Don't rely on just one travel site. Prices can vary across different platforms. Use meta-search engines like Kayak, Skyscanner, or Google Flights to compare prices across various sites.

- **Sign Up for Alerts**: Many travel sites and apps allow you to set up price alerts for specific routes or hotels. This way, you'll be notified when prices drop.

- **Check Alternative Airports or Locations:** Sometimes, flying into a smaller, nearby airport or staying in a hotel a bit further from the city center can be cheaper. Consider the cost and convenience of transportation to your final destination if you choose this option.

- **Consider Package Deals:** Sometimes, booking a flight, hotel, and car rental together can be cheaper than booking them separately. Look for package deals on travel sites.

- **Use Cashback and Reward Programs:** If you have a credit card offering travel rewards or cashback, take advantage of it. If you travel frequently, join airline and hotel loyalty programs.

- **Check the Airline or Hotel Website Directly:** After finding a good deal on a third-party site, check the airline or hotel's own website. Sometimes, they offer a lower price or better conditions (like free cancellation or breakfast).

The algorithms powering travel sites are complex systems that provide a seamless and personalized booking experience. They balance supply and demand, adjust prices dynamically, rank search results to match user preferences and optimize the overall user experience. As technology evolves, these algorithms will become even more sophisticated, further transforming how we plan and book our travels. However, ethical considerations must guide these advancements to ensure fairness and transparency in travel booking.

Compare, Compare, Compare

Dive into the ocean of travel sites, each with its quirks. Booking.com adjusts its prices based on various factors, so dig deep for limited-time offers or secret deals. Travelocity.com, with its Price Match Guarantee, invites adventure. Did you find a better deal elsewhere? They might match it. Expedia.com is your budget-friendly genie, offering "Deal of the Day" that might make your Parisian dream a click away. Kayak.com helps you navigate the vast sea of options with its flexible date search to find the best fares. Don't overlook Skyscanner and Google Flights for a broader perspective on available deals; remember, loyalty programs can offer exclusive deals and perks.

The Secret Sauce: Local Alternatives

While major travel sites are great, local French booking sites and tourism websites might have hidden deals. For a truly authentic Parisian experience, consider staying in a local apartment or guesthouse. Websites like Airbnb, HomeAway, and VRBO are your gateways to unique accommodations, many of which are offered as part of package deals for significant savings.

Empowering the Traveler

Armed with these tips, you can outsmart travel algorithms. Be flexible with your dates, explore different neighborhoods, and immerse yourself in the local culture. Remember, safety and sustainability are key. Consider travel insurance and eco-friendly travel options. Don't overlook the importance of insurance for peace of mind. A little knowledge of local customs goes a long way, and basic French phrases like "Bonjour", "Merci", and "S'il vous plaît" can open many doors.

Chapter 7

Should you pay for private museum tours?

This book, a tribute to the love for museums, is crafted for those who share a passion beyond just liking them. My twenties were joyously spent volunteering at the National Gallery of Art, a place I cherish deeply. Museums are my vacation sanctuaries.

My approach to travel mirrors that of a private tour guide. I meticulously review each museum's website and map, curating a list of highlights. I delve into the background of each piece, ensuring the inclusion of family preferences. With varied tastes in our group, ranging from modern art to decorative arts and period antiques, I strive to cater to all.

However, organizing such trips can be overwhelming, especially when visiting six museums in a single journey. Balancing a detailed plan with spontaneity is key. I utilize audio guides and museum websites to optimize our experience.

Though I seldom opt for private museum tours, I once considered one in the Marais district, which unfortunately didn't materialize. Tours in specific areas differ from those in a place like the Louvre, where private guides offer distinct advantages.

This chapter delves into the merits of private museum tours in Paris, particularly beneficial for families with elderly members or young children. While not my usual preference, it's an option worth exploring for readers.

Tailored Experience for All Ages

Private museum tours are a great way to tailor your experience, especially if you are traveling with kids or older relatives. Unlike group tours, private tours can be customized to suit the interests and preferences of the participants. This means you can skip the sections that don't interest you and spend more time in the areas that fascinate you. For example, if you are traveling with kids, you can opt for a tour that focuses on the museum's interactive exhibits, where they can learn and have fun at the same time. Similarly, if you are traveling with older relatives, you can choose a less physically demanding and informative tour, where they can sit and listen to the guide's stories.

Personalized Attention

Private museum tours offer personalized attention from a knowledgeable guide. The guide can provide in-depth insights into the museum's collections, history, and architecture. They can answer your questions, share anecdotes, and provide a deeper understanding of the artworks on display.

Unlike group tours, where the guide has to cater to the needs of a large group, a private tour allows for one-on-one interaction with the guide. This means you can take your time admiring the artwork, asking questions, and getting personalized attention from the guide.

Avoid Crowds and Long Queues

Paris museums are popular tourist destinations, attracting large crowds throughout the year. This means that you may have to wait in long queues to enter the museum, and once inside, you may have to jostle through the crowds to get a glimpse of the artwork. Private museum tours offer the advantage of skipping the long queues and entering the museum without delay. This means you can spend more time admiring the artwork and waiting less in queues. Additionally, private tours can be scheduled during off-peak hours, when the museum is less crowded, ensuring a more comfortable and enjoyable experience.

Flexible Schedule

Private museum tours offer the flexibility of choosing your date and time. Unlike group tours, which have fixed schedules, private tours can be scheduled at a convenient time. This means you can plan your visit to the museum according to your schedule without worrying about missing out on the tour. Additionally, private tours can be customized to fit your itinerary, allowing you to visit multiple museums in a single day or spend more time in a single museum.

Unique Experiences

Private museum tours offer unique experiences that are not possible with group tours. For example, some private tours offer access to areas of the museum that are not open to the public, such as the museum's conservation lab or storage area. This provides a rare opportunity to see the artworks up close and learn about their preservation and restoration. Similarly, some private tours offer the opportunity to meet with museum curators, artists, or collectors, providing exclusive insight into the museum's collections.

Quality Time with Family and Friends

Private museum tours offer quality time with family and friends. Unlike group tours, which may include strangers, private tours are exclusively for you and your companions. This means that you can enjoy the museum's collections in the company of your loved ones, sharing your thoughts and opinions and creating memories that will last a lifetime. Private tours offer an intimate and relaxed setting where you can engage in meaningful conversations with your loved ones while admiring the artwork. Additionally, private tours can be customized to suit the interests and preferences of your companions, ensuring that everyone has a memorable experience.

Accessibility for All

Private museum tours offer accessibility for all, including those with disabilities or special needs. Private tours can be customized to cater to individuals with mobility issues, visual impairments, or other disabilities. The guide can assist, such as wheelchair access, audio guides, or sign language interpreters, ensuring everyone can enjoy the museum's collections. Additionally, private tours offer a quieter and less overwhelming environment, which can benefit individuals with sensory processing issues.

Value for Money

Private museum tours may seem expensive initially, but they offer value for money. Private tours offer personalized attention from a knowledgeable guide, skip-the-line access, and the flexibility of choosing your schedule. Additionally, private tours can be customized to suit your budget, allowing you to choose the tour that fits your needs and preferences. Private tours also offer the opportunity to see the museum's collections in a unique and exclusive setting, which may not be possible with group tours.

Cultural Immersion

Private museum tours offer cultural immersion, allowing you to experience the museum's collections more deeply and meaningfully. The guide can provide insights into the museum's history, architecture, and cultural significance, providing a deeper understanding of the displayed artworks. Additionally, private tours can be customized to include local traditions, such as visiting a nearby market or tasting local cuisine, providing a holistic cultural experience.

Private museum tours offer numerous benefits, including a tailored experience for all ages, personalized attention, skip-the-line access, flexibility, unique experiences, quality time with family and friends, accessibility, value for money, and cultural immersion. If planning to visit Paris museums, consider booking a private tour to ensure a memorable and enjoyable experience.

Chapter 8

The Arrondissement System

The arrondissements of Paris, a distinctive feature of the city's administrative landscape, represent a unique amalgamation of history, urban planning, and governance. This chapter delves into the intricacies of these arrondissements, shedding light on their formation, structure, and role in the fabric of Parisian life.

Paris, the iconic capital of France, is situated within the Île-de-France region and functions as both a city and a department in its own right. The concept of arrondissements, administrative districts that Paris is divided into, plays a crucial role in the city's governance and organization. As of 2009, Paris had a population of approximately 2,234,105 people, spread across 105 square kilometers, resulting in a high population density of around 21,000 per square kilometer.

The arrondissements of Paris are not only administrative units but also hold significant cultural and historical value. There are 20 districts, each with a unique character and identity, often tied to local landmarks or historical events. For instance, the 5th arrondissement is colloquially known as "Panthéon," referencing the famous building within its boundaries. The arrondissements are numbered distinctively, with the last two digits in most Parisian postal codes (ranging from 75001 to 75020) indicating the arrondissement number. Knowing this information will immediately let you know where you are heading, as most addresses posted online include the postal code. For example, the Musée du Louvre, 75001, Paris, France. The postal code is 75001, meaning the Musée is located in the first arrondissement.

The spatial arrangement of the arrondissements is particularly fascinating. They are set out in a clockwise spiral, often likened to a snail shell, starting from the city's center. This arrangement is a quirky detail and a well-thought-out urban design that dates back to the 19th century. The first arrondissement begins on the Right Bank of the Seine River, and the sequence continues clockwise. This design aids in both navigation and administrative efficiency.

Governance within these arrondissements is a unique aspect of Parisian administration. Paris is the only French city that is both a municipality and a department, a status that has significant implications for its administrative structure. The governance of Paris is influenced by the PLM Law of 1982, a legislative framework that redefined the governance of Paris, Lyon, and Marseille. Under this law, Paris has a city council known as the Council of Paris and 20 arrondissement councils. However, the powers vested in these arrondissement councils are relatively limited compared to those of the city council.

Each arrondissement is subdivided into four quartiers (neighborhoods), resulting in 80 quartiers in Paris. This subdivision further enhances local governance and ensures that the needs and issues of smaller communities within each arrondissement are addressed effectively.

The history of Paris's arrondissements is as rich and intricate as the city itself. The initial division of Paris into arrondissements occurred on 11 October 1795, when the city was divided into twelve arrondissements. These were numbered from west to east, with numbers 1 to 9 located on the Right Bank of the Seine and 10 to 12 on the Left Bank. These arrondissements were subdivided into four quartiers, aligning with the 48 original districts created in 1790.

However, the modern arrangement of 20 arrondissements emerged from the ambitious urban planning under Emperor Napoleon III and Baron Haussmann, the Prefect of the Seine. In the late 1850s, a plan was developed to incorporate several surrounding communes into Paris. This expansion, legislated in 1859 and implemented in 1860, led to the restructuring of the arrondissement system. The original twelve arrondissements were reorganized, and eight new ones were added, bringing the total to twenty. This reorganization was not merely an administrative change but a significant transformation that reshaped Paris's urban landscape.

The peculiar numbering of the arrondissements in a spiral pattern was a strategic choice. This system was proposed by Jean-Frédéric Possoz, the mayor of Passy, one of the communes incorporated into Paris. His idea was to start the numbering on the Right Bank, which placed Passy in the 16th arrondissement, a more prestigious designation than the 13th, which residents initially objected to. This numbering also shifted the focus to the central areas of Paris, including the Louvre and Tuileries Palace, which became part of the 1st arrondissement.

The arrondissements of Paris are not just administrative divisions but are emblematic of the city's rich history and dynamic urban landscape. They reflect the evolution of Paris from a medieval city to a modern metropolis, embodying the cultural, historical, and administrative complexities of one of the world's most renowned cities. The arrondissements are a testament to Paris's ability to adapt and grow while preserving its heritage and identity, making them an integral part of the city's charm and appeal.

Chapter 9

Your Temporary Paris Home

I recommend staying in the 8th Arrondissement, or the Élysée, located on the right bank of the River Seine in Paris for your first trip. It is one of the city's most affluent and prestigious districts, known for its luxury shops, high-end hotels, and upscale restaurants. The area covers 3.88 km² and is home to some of the city's most famous landmarks, including the Champs-Élysées and the Arc de Triomphe.

The history of the 8th Arrondissement dates back to the 17th century when the area was primarily rural and dotted with small villages and farms. In the 18th century, the district began to develop as a fashionable residential area for the city's aristocracy, who built grand mansions and townhouses.

During the French Revolution, many of these properties were confiscated and sold off to the highest bidder, leading to a decline in the area's prestige. It wasn't until the mid-19th century that the district regained its status as a fashionable residential area, thanks partly to the construction of the Champs-Élysées in the 1830s.

The Champs-Élysées quickly became one of the most popular places to see and be seen in Paris, with its wide tree-lined avenue, theaters, and cafés attracting the city's elite. In the late 19th and early 20th centuries, the area became even more fashionable with the opening of luxury hotels such as the Ritz Paris, the Crillon, and the Arc de Triomphe construction.

During World War II, the 8th Arrondissement was heavily bombed, resulting in significant damage to many of the area's buildings. However, the district was quickly rebuilt after the war, and many historic buildings and landmarks were restored to their former glory.

Today, the 8th Arrondissement is one of the most popular tourist destinations in Paris, with millions of visitors flocking to the area each year to shop, dine, and take in the sights. It is home to some of the city's most famous luxury brands, including Louis Vuitton, Chanel, and Dior, as well as many high-end restaurants and cafés.

In addition to its shopping and dining options, the 8th Arrondissement is also known for its many museums and cultural institutions, including the Grand Palais and the Petit Palais. The district is also home to the Élysée Palace, the official residence of the President of the French Republic.

The 8th Arrondissement has a rich and fascinating history that spans several centuries. From its beginnings as a rural district to its status as one of the most affluent and prestigious areas of Paris, the district has played a significant role in the city's development and continues to be a popular destination for tourists and locals alike. It will make a great home for you while you explore Paris, and it is a central transit hub where you can breeze around the city on buses or trains.

OK, so where to stay?

Paris has many hotels, ranging from budget-friendly to luxurious and high-end establishments. Many hotels in Paris are housed in historic buildings, adding to the city's charm and character. The city's hotels typically offer a range of amenities, including air conditioning, Wi-Fi, room service, and breakfast. Some hotels also offer on-site restaurants, bars, and fitness facilities. I recommend two American-friendly hotels, the first in the 16th and the other in the 8th arrondissements. Both hotels are great value for the money and are centrally located. I stayed at the Hotel Pley on my most recent trip and was delighted with the location, room quality, and service.

Ultimately, wherever you choose, you must consider many factors, including price, proximity to transit, a super-market, a pharmacy, a good bakery, and laundry facilities if needed. I personally don't care about buffet breakfast, room service, or business services. I want a clean, modern room with good lighting and a nice bed. I don't want to pay for anything else, nor should you.

Please consider the following tips before booking a hotel. Firstly, check the major booking sites for the best package deals, which might help you save significantly by buying your airfare with your hotel. Secondly, try contacting the hotel through their website to see if you can get an even better deal. It may not always work, but it's worth a few moments to check.

Lastly, before making the final decision, it's a good idea to look at TikTok and YouTube to see if previous guests have posted tours of the hotel and their rooms. These videos can provide valuable insights into the hotel and the surrounding neighborhood. However, look at multiple videos, as some may be videos from influencers who are given free accommodation in exchange for their video.

Hôtel Victor Hugo

The hotel in the fashionable 16th district of Paris, at 19 rue Copernic, 75016, is a great option. Hugo is near various shopping centers, restaurants, and famous landmarks such as the Place du Trocadéro, the Eiffel Tower, the Champs-Élysée, and the Arc de Triomphe. You can easily stroll to these prestigious locations from your hotel and explore the typically Parisian neighborhood with its various cafés, restaurants, and shops. Whether traveling for business, tourism, shopping, French gastronomy, shows, or entertainment, you will find everything you need for a good price.

Hotel Pley

The PLEY Hotel is in the heart of Paris, only a few minutes from the Champs-Élysées at 214 rue du Faubourg Saint-Honoré. It is a lively and vibrant place that provides a vintage atmosphere. The hotel's decor is inspired by the rich radio history of the 8th district of Paris, which makes it unique and original.

You can discover fragments of the hotel's past through archival photographs of the radio Europe 1 and advertising posters from that period. Take the time to admire the old radio sets found on the roads of France or the works of the contemporary artist Julien Nédélec. The PLEY Hotel pays homage to the history of French radio, which had its greatest moments written in the streets of this neighborhood.

Overall, the Hotel Pley in Paris has unique characteristics, but it is best to check its website or online reviews to better understand what the hotel offers.

Chapter 10

Paris Café Culture

Parisian café culture is integral to the city's identity and lifestyle. This cultural phenomenon has been a part of Paris's history for centuries and continues to thrive today. Whether you're sipping espresso at a sidewalk café or enjoying a croissant while reading a book, Parisian cafés offer a unique and charming experience that is quintessentially French.

One of the defining characteristics of Parisian cafés is their ambiance. The interior design of many cafés is often stylish and chic, featuring classic French decor and furnishings. Many cafés have a cozy, intimate atmosphere, soft lighting, and comfortable seating. French music playing in the background often complements the ambiance, creating a relaxed and romantic atmosphere.

Another defining characteristic of Parisian cafés is their outdoor seating. Many cafés have tables and chairs on the sidewalk, allowing customers to sit outside and enjoy the sights and sounds of the city. Outdoor seating is particularly popular in the spring and summer when the weather is warm and sunny. Sitting outside at a Parisian café is a great way to people-watch, soak up the atmosphere, and enjoy a leisurely meal or drink.

Cafés in Paris are not just places to eat and drink but also hubs for socializing and intellectual discussion. Parisian cafés have a long history of attracting writers, artists, and intellectuals who gather to discuss ideas and share their work. Famous writers such as Ernest Hemingway and Simone de Beauvoir were known to frequent Parisian cafés. The intellectual and artistic community has long been a part of the city's identity, and the cafés have played a significant role in fostering this community.

Parisian cafés offer a wide range of food and drinks, from classic French pastries to gourmet coffee and wine. Croissants, baguettes, and macarons are some of the most popular French pastries in cafés. Coffee is also an important part of the café culture, and many cafés serve espresso, cappuccino, and café au lait. Wine is also a popular choice, and many cafés offer a variety of red, white, and rose wines. Parisian cafés offer food and drink options that are often high-quality and reflect the city's reputation for gourmet cuisine.

One of the most iconic Parisian cafés is Café de Flore. Located in the Saint-Germain-des-Prés neighborhood, Café de Flore has been a gathering place for writers, artists, and intellectuals since it opened in 1887. The café has an elegant interior featuring red velvet chairs, mirrored walls, and a stunning art deco bar. It is known for its excellent coffee and pastries and is a must-visit destination for anyone interested in experiencing Parisian café culture.

Paris is famous for its iconic cafés, including Café de Flore and Les Deux Magots. These cafés have a rich history and were frequented by famous writers and intellectuals such as Jean-Paul Sartre and Ernest Hemingway. Les Deux Magots has a stunning Art Nouveau interior and an outdoor terrace that offers breathtaking views of Saint-Germain-des-Prés. The café is known for its excellent coffee and hot chocolate and is a popular destination for both locals and tourists.

Aside from these iconic cafés, Paris has many other notable cafés that offer a unique and charming experience. La Palette, also located in the Saint-Germain-des-Prés neighborhood, is another historic café that has been a gathering place for artists and intellectuals since the early 20th century. The café has an intimate atmosphere is famous for its excellent wine selection. Another notable café is Café Marly, located in the Louvre Museum. The café has a stunning terrace that overlooks the iconic glass pyramid and offers a luxurious dining experience.

Parisian cafés represent the city's identity and way of life. They are not just places to eat and drink but also to relax, socialize, and enjoy Paris's beauty and culture. Parisian cafés are essential to the city's history and have significantly shaped its cultural identity. They offer a unique and charming experience that is quintessentially French and should not be missed by anyone visiting the city.

Paris café culture is integral to the city's identity and lifestyle, offering a unique and charming experience quintessentially French, from sipping espresso at a sidewalk café to enjoying a croissant and reading a book. They are a place to relax, socialize, and take in the beauty and culture of Paris. The ambiance of Parisian cafés is often stylish and chic, featuring classic French decor and furnishings. Many cafés have a cozy, intimate atmosphere, soft lighting, and comfortable seating. Outdoor seating is also popular, particularly in the spring and summer months. Parisian cafés are places to eat and drink and a hub for socializing and intellectual discussion. Famous writers and intellectuals have long been drawn to Parisian cafés, significantly fostering the city's intellectual and artistic community. Parisian cafés offer a wide range of food and drinks, from classic French pastries to gourmet coffee and wine. They are an important part of the city's reputation for gourmet cuisine. Finally, Parisian cafés symbolize the city's identity and way of life. They are an important part of the city's history and cultural identity and should not be missed by anyone visiting Paris.

If you want to understand French culture, I recommend you dine at a local café or brasserie once daily. Personally, I prefer to eat light during the day and then enjoy a meal at a brasserie at night.

But what exactly is the difference between a brasserie, bistro, and a café? A bistro is a small neighborhood restaurant that is usually more affordable. A brasserie typically serves traditional French fare all day and night. A café, on the other hand, is a place for coffee and light food or small plates. Generally, you sit inside for a meal and have light food in street cafés. If you're looking for a place to eat out, you can use food apps like TheFork (thefork.fr) to look at the menus or Google to get a sense of how much you'll spend.

In my family, we have three different dietary restrictions to consider. One person can't eat wheat, one is a vegetarian, and another can't have beef or dairy. Traveling with these restrictions is challenging, so we always check before going to a bistro. We often opt for vegan food when it's reliably available, but in Paris, this might not be possible for every meal.

Parisian cafés can be found throughout the city, from the bustling streets of the Latin Quarter to the historic districts of Le Marais and Montmartre. They are a place to relax, socialize, and take in the beauty and culture of Paris. Parisian cafés are more than just a place to grab a quick bite or a cup of coffee; they are a cultural institution that has become an integral part of the city's way of life.

Chapter 11

Flea Markets, Antiques, and Thrift

Paris is known for its fashion and style, but city shopping can be expensive. However, there are ways to score great deals and find unique pieces without breaking the bank. One great option for those looking for bargains is to head to the city's flea markets and thrift stores. For locations of Paris flea markets for the week, check out Alicja Kissaa on TikTok (https://www.tiktok.com/@alicjakissaa), who posts the updated market list and videos of her shopping finds.

If you have a bit more in your budget and are looking for consignment shopping, try Bobby Paris (bobbyparis.com) at 89 rue Réaumur, 75002 Paris. There will be seasonal finds from recent ready-to-wear stores and designers. People swear by the designer bargains. Check their Instagram before going for any updates.

Another option for thrift and vintage shopping in Paris is to check out the many secondhand shops and thrift stores located throughout the city. These shops offer pre-loved clothing and accessories at prices that won't break the bank. One of the most popular thrift stores in Paris is FREE'P'STAR, which has several locations throughout the city. Here, you can find an eclectic mix of vintage and retro clothing, accessories, shoes, and more.

Another great option is Kilo Shop, which has a unique pricing system. Instead of paying for individual items, you pay by the weight. You can fill a bag with as many items as possible and pay a flat rate per kilogram. This is a great way to score some amazing vintage clothing and accessories for a steal.

The King Of Frip is another popular thrift store in Paris, with a great selection of vintage and secondhand clothing. This store is known for its affordable prices and trendy pieces, making it a popular destination for fashion-forward shoppers on a budget.

Hippy Market is the place for you if you want something more bohemian. This shop offers a wide range of vintage and bohemian-inspired clothing and accessories, including flowy dresses, fringe jackets, and oversized sunglasses.

Noir Kennedy is another great vintage store in Paris. It offers a wide range of clothing, accessories, and home decor. This store is known for its unique pieces and edgy aesthetic, making it a great destination for those looking to add some edge to their wardrobe.

Most of these thrift stores and vintage shops can be found off the 1 train at Hotel de Ville down to St Paul of the same line. It's a good idea to make a loop and spend time browsing, as you never know what hidden gems you might find. Some stores have changing rooms, while others do not, so be sure to bring a tape measure and write down your European sizes on a card or your phone.

In addition to the flea markets and thrift stores, several vintage and secondhand clothing markets in Paris are held annually. These markets combine dozens of vendors selling vintage and pre-loved clothing, accessories, and more. One of the most popular markets is the Vintage Clothing Kilo Sale, held several times a year in different locations throughout the city.

If you are looking for antique flea markets, there are some in Paris, but if you can take a bus or a train about a half hour outside the city, you will not be disappointed.

- Marché aux Puces de Saint-Ouen, 110 rue des Rosiers, 93400 Saint-Ouen-sur-Seine, France (pucesdeparis-saintouen.com)

- Marché Dauphine, 132-140 rue des Rosiers, 93400 Saint-Ouen-sur-Seine, France (marche-dauphine.com/en)

- Marché Biron, 85 rue des Rosiers, 93400 Saint-Ouen-sur-Seine, France (marchebiron.com)

- Paul Bert Serpette, 110 rue des Rosiers, 93400 Saint-Ouen-sur-Seine, France (paulbert-serpette.com/en)

Overall, shopping in Paris doesn't have to be expensive. You can score amazing deals on unique and stylish clothing and accessories with research and savvy shopping skills. Whether you're into vintage fashion or looking for affordable pieces to add to your wardrobe, there's something for everyone in Paris.

Always check to see the hours before you go:

FREE'P'STAR
93 rue de la Verrerie 75004 Paris
instagram.com/freepstar_officiel/?hl=en

Noir Kennedy
22 rue du Roi de Sicile, 75004 Paris
instagram.com/noirkennedyofficiel/

Hippy Market
41 rue du Temple, 75004 Paris
hippy-market.fr

The King of Frip
33 rue du Roi de Sicile, 75004 Paris
frippy.co/fr/magasins/paris/the-king-of-frip

Kilo Shop Kawaii
65 rue de la Verrerie, 75004 Paris
kilo-shop.com

Tilt Vintage 4th
8 rue de Rivoli, 75004 Paris (multiple locations)
tilt-vintage.com

Bottega Concept Store
11 Bd des Filles du Calvaire, 75003 Paris
bottega-vintage-concept-store.business.site

Kiliwatch
64 rue Tiquetonne, 75002 Paris
instagram.com/kiliwatch.paris/?hl=en

Vintage 77
77 rue de Ménilmontant, 75020 Paris
facebook.com/p/Vintage-77-M%C3%A9nilmontant-
Paris-75020-100063652654900/

KiloShop
125 Bd Saint-Germain, 75006 Paris (multiple locations)
kilo-shop.com

Gudule
72 rue Saint-André des Arts, 75006 Paris
gudule.com/boutique-gudule

Chapter 12

Lots of Museums in Paris

Paris has a rich history and culture, and there are many museums to choose from. While the Louvre and the Musée d'Orsay are worth visiting, many smaller, niche museums offer a more unique and intimate experience. Make sure that you check the museum's website well before the visit. Some have posted fees, and some do not. Many have unusual open days or hours. Remember, you can tell what arrondissement the museum is in by using the last two digits of the zip code. So, if you're looking for a more unique and intimate museum experience in Paris, then be sure to check out some of the smaller niche museums. You won't be disappointed.

The big museums in Paris can be very crowded, especially during peak season. A miniature museum is a great option if you're looking for a more relaxed and enjoyable museum experience.

Smaller museums often focus on a specific topic or artist, which can give you a deeper understanding of that subject. For example, the Musée Rodin is dedicated to the work of a famous sculptor, while the Musée de la Vie Romantique explores the lives and careers of artists and writers from the Romantic era.

Many smaller museums, such as Montmartre or the Marais, are located in charming settings. This allows you to explore these areas and experience Paris.

Many visitors find themselves floating by art at the Louvre as if in a lazy river flowing by art that becomes scenery. So, if you only have a few hours free, visiting a small museum will let you dive into a particular type of art for a deeper understanding.

Art Ludique (Temporarily Closed) Contemporary art exhibitions in comic books, manga, cinema, live animation, and video games. Announcements suggest that Ludique will be moved to the Saint-Lazare Station. *Website: artludique.com.*

Bibliothèque-Musée de l'Opéra National de Paris Palais Garnier, 8 rue Scribe, 75009 Paris. Library and museum about the Paris Opera, part of the Music Department of the National Library of France. *Website: bnf.fr/fr/opera.*

Bibliothèque Polonaise de Paris 6 Quai d'Orléans, 75004 Paris. The Polish Library in Paris, managed by the Polish Historical and Literary Society, has been a center of Polish emigration since the middle of the 19th century and the largest cultural institution representing Poland outside the borders of this state. *Website: bibliotheque-polonaise-paris-shlp.fr/.*

Bibliothèque Nationale de France There are five branches. Richelieu: 58 rue de Richelieu - 75002 Paris, François-Mitterrand: Quai François Mauriac, 75706 Paris, Arsenal: 1 rue de Sully – 75004 Paris. Jean-Vilar: 8 rue de Mons – 84000 Avignon, and Opéra: 8 rue Scribe - 75009 Paris. Day passes are required, so check the website for details and prices. *Website: bnf.fr/fr.*

Catacombes de Paris 1 Av. du Colonel Henri Rol-Tanguy, 75014 Paris. Underground ossuary with the remains of over six million people. Spiral staircase up and down. *Website: catacombes.paris.fr.*

Cité de l'Architecture et du Patrimoine 1 Pl. du Trocadéro et du 11 Novembre, 75116 Paris. Architecture Located in the Palais de Chaillot includes Musée National des Monuments Français with plaster casts of French architecture, a gallery of reproduced wall paintings, stained-glass windows from historical monuments, and French and international architecture from 1850 to the present. *Website: citedelarchitecture.fr/fr.*

Cité des Sciences et de l'Industrie 30 Av. Corentin Cariou, 75019 Paris. Hands-on science exhibits. *Website: cite-sciences.fr/fr/accueil.*

Cité nationale de l'histoire de l'immigration 12th. Palais de la Porte Dorée, 293 Av. Daumesnil, 75012 Paris, France. History and culture of immigration in France from the 19th century to the present, located in the Palais de la Porte Dorée. *Website: histoire-immigration.fr.*

Espace Dalí 18th. 11 rue Poulbot, 75018 Paris. The Espace Dalí is a permanent exhibition in France devoted to Salvador Dalí consisting mainly of sculptures and engravings. Near the Place du Tertre in the Montmartre district of Paris, the museum has around 300 original artworks. *Website: daliparis.com.*

Fondation Cartier pour l'Art Contemporain 14th. 261 Bd Raspail, 75014 Paris. The Fondation Cartier pour l'Art Contemporain, known simply as the Fondation Cartier, is a contemporary art museum. *Website: fondationcartier.com/en/.*

Fondation Custodia 7th. 121 rue de Lille, 75007 Paris. Frits Lugt's collection of European drawings, prints, paintings, books, and artists' letters from the 15th to 19th century focuses on Dutch and Flemish Old Masters, as well as Italian and French artists. *Website: fondationcustodia.fr.*

Fondation Jean Dubuffet 6th. 137 rue de Sèvres, 75006 Paris. Works by Jean Dubuffet. Hours are short daily, and the museum is closed in August. *Website: dubuffetfondation.com.*

Fondation Louis Vuitton 8 Av. du Mahatma Gandhi, 75116 Paris. The Louis Vuitton Foundation, previously Louis Vuitton Foundation for Creation, is a French art museum and cultural center sponsored by the LVMH and its subsidiaries. It is run as a legally separate, nonprofit entity as part of LVMH's promotion of art and culture. This is not a museum about purses. *Website: fondationlouisvuitton.fr.*

Gaîté Lyrique 3bis rue Papin, 75003 Paris. Modern performance venue with a stately 19th-century façade & many events & workshops. Check the website before you go. *Website: gaite-lyrique.net.*

Galerie des Gobelins (Temporarily Closed) 42 Av. des Gobelins, 75013 Paris. The Gobelins Manufactory is a historic tapestry factory in Paris, France. The Manufacture Nationale des Gobelins is open but at a different address. It is located at 42 avenue des Gobelins, near Les Gobelins métro station in the 13th arrondissement of Paris. It was originally established on the site as a medieval dyeing business by the Gobelin family. *Website: mobiliernational.culture.gouv.fr/fr.*

Galerie nationale du Jeu de Paume 1 Pl. de la Concorde, 75008 Paris. Jeu de Paume is an arts center for modern and postmodern photography and media. It is located in the north corner of the Tuileries Gardens next to the Place de la Concorde. *Website: jeudepaume.org.*

Galeries nationales du Grand Palais (Temporary Closed) 8th. 2 Pl. Joffre, 75007 Paris. The Galleries Nationales du Grand Palais are museum spaces located in the Grand Palais in the 8th arrondissement of Paris. They serve as home to major art exhibits and cultural events. A small part of the collection can be viewed at the Grand-Palais Éphémère. *Website: grandpalais.fr/fr/lieux/grand-palais-ephemere.*

Henri Cartier-Bresson Foundation 79 rue des Archives, 75003 Paris. The Henri Cartier-Bresson Foundation, also known as Fondation HCB, is an art gallery and non-profit organization in Paris that was established to preserve and show the work of Henri Cartier-Bresson and Martine Franck, and the work of others. *Website: henricartierbresson.org.*

Institut Tessin or Institut suédois 1 rue Payenne, 75003 Paris. The Institut Tessin, also known as the Centre Culturel suédois, is a museum in Paris dedicated to the history of Franco-Swedish artistic exchanges. *Website: paris.si.se/en/.*

Maison d'Auguste Comte 10 rue Monsieur le Prince, 75006 Paris. Historic house with restored 19th-century period rooms of positivist philosopher Auguste Comte (1798–1857), one of the 32 Maisons des illustres (cultural heritage site) in the region Île de France. *Website: augustecomte.org.*

Maison de Balzac 47 rue Raynouard, 75016 Paris. The Maison de Balzac is a writer's house museum in the former residence of French novelist Honoré de Balzac. *Website: maisondebalzac.paris.fr.*

Maison Européenne de la Photographie (La MEP) 5/7 rue de Fourcy, 75004 Paris. The Maison Européenne de la Photographie, located in the historic heart of Paris, is a center for contemporary photographic art and opened in February 1996. *Website: mep-fr.org.*

Maison de Victor Hugo 6 Place des Vosges, 75004 Paris. The Maison de Victor Hugo is a writer's house museum. It's where Victor Hugo lived for 16 years between 1832 and 1848. The museum is decorated with original furniture, artifacts, and sketches. *Website: maisonsvictorhugo.paris.fr.*

Maison La Roche 8-10 Sq. du Dr Blanche, 75016 Paris. Villa La Roche, also Maison La Roche, is a house in Paris, designed by Le Corbusier and his cousin Pierre Jeanneret in 1923–1925. It was designed for Raoul La Roche, a Swiss banker from Basel and collector of avant-garde art. Villa La Roche now houses the Fondation Le Corbusier. *Website: fondationlecorbusier.fr.*

Maxim's Art Nouveau "Collection 1900" (Currently Closed) 3 rue Royale, 75008 Paris. Maxim's Art Nouveau "Collection 1900", also known as the Musée Art Nouveau - Maxim's is a private collection of Art Nouveau objects and decor, located in the 8th arrondissement above Maxim's Paris restaurant. *Website: maxims-de-paris.com/fr/le-musee.*

Mémorial de la Shoah 17 rue Geoffroy l'Asnier, 75004 Paris. Mémorial de la Shoah is the Holocaust museum in Paris, France. The memorial is in the 4th arrondissement of Paris, in the Marais district, which had a large Jewish population at the beginning of World War II. The memorial was opened by President Jacques Chirac, on 27 January 2005. *Website: memorialdelashoah.org.*

Minerals collection of Pierre and Marie Curie University, Sorbonne University 4 Place Jussieu, 75005 Paris. The mineralogy collection of the Pierre and Marie Curie University (mineralogy and crystallography laboratory) displays 2,000 samples from all over the world, selected from among the most beautiful and important minerals in the earth sciences and those in use in industry and the arts. *Website: collection-mineraux.sorbonne-universite.fr.*

Mundolingua 10 rue Servandoni, 75006 Paris. Mundolingua is a museum situated in the 6th arrondissement of Paris. Its purpose is to present information, objects, and documents relating to language, linguistic diversity, and linguistics to the general public. *Website: mundolingua.org.*

Musée Adzak 3 rue Jonquoy, 75014 Paris. Art exhibits, paintings, sculpture, and photography by a wide range of artists. *Website: N/A.*

Musée "Bible et Terre Sainte" (Currently closed) 6th. Catholic Institute of Paris, 21 rue d'Assas, 75006 Paris. Archaeological artifacts arranged to show everyday life in Palestine from 5000 BCE to 600 CE. This is a very small museum. *Website: bibleterresainte.wordpress.com/le-musee.*

Musée Baccarat 11 Place des Etats-Unis 75116 Paris, Decorative art Baccarat fine glass work, including vases, dishes and stemware, and limited-edition collections. *Website: us.baccarat.com/en/museums.*

Musée Bourdelle 18 rue Antoine Bourdelle, 75015 Paris. The Musée Bourdelle is an art museum in the French sculptor Antoine Bourdelle studio. *Website: bourdelle.paris.fr.*

Musée Carnavalet 23 rue de Sévigné, 75003 Paris. The Musée Carnavalet in Paris is dedicated to the history of the city. The museum occupies two neighboring mansions: the Hôtel Carnavalet and the former Hôtel Le Peletier de Saint Fargeau. *Website: carnavalet.paris.fr.*

Musée Cernuschi 8th. 7 Av. Velasquez, 75008 Paris, France. The Musée Cernuschi, officially also the Musée des arts de l'Asie de la Ville de Paris, is an Asian art museum located at 7 avenue Vélasquez, near Parc Monceau, in Paris, France. Its Asian art collection is second in Paris only to that of the Musée Guimet. *Website: cernuschi.paris.fr/en.*

Musée Clemenceau 16th. 8 rue Benjamin Franklin, 75116 Paris, France. Historic house apartment and garden of Georges Clemenceau (1841–1929), French statesman and writer. *Website: musee-clemenceau.fr.*

Musée Cognacq-Jay 3rd. 8 rue Elzevir, 75003 Paris, France. The Musée Cognacq-Jay is a museum located in the Hôtel Donon in the 3rd arrondissement of Paris. The museum's collection was formed between 1900 and 1925 by Théodore-Ernest Cognacq and his wife Marie-Louise Jaÿ, founders of La Samaritaine department store. *Website: museecognacq-jay.paris.fr.*

Musée Curie 1 rue Pierre et Marie Curie, 75005 Paris. Science History of radiology research and the work of Pierre and Marie Curie. *Website: musee.curie.fr.*

Musée d'Art et d'Histoire du Judaïsme Hôtel de Saint-Aignan, 71 rue du Temple, 75003 Paris. The Musée d'Art et d'Histoire du Judaïsme or mahJ is the largest French museum of Jewish art and history. It is located in the Hôtel de Saint-Aignan in the Marais district in Paris. The museum conveys the rich history and culture of Jews in Europe and North Africa from the Middle Ages to the 20th century. *Website: mahj.org/fr.*

Musée d'Art Moderne de la Ville de Paris 11 Av. du Président Wilson, 75116 Paris. Musée d'Art Moderne de Paris or MAM Paris, is a major municipal museum dedicated to modern and contemporary art of the 20th and 21st centuries, including monumental murals by Raoul Dufy, Gaston Suisse, and Henri Matisse. *Website: mam.paris.fr.*

Musée d'Art Naïf – Max Fourny 15 rue de la mairie, 78490 Vicq. Near Paris, in the heart of Yvelines, in a charming 18th-century farm, the Vicq Museum of Naive Art in Ile-de-France houses a collection of more than 1,400 works from more than 55 countries and all continents. *Website: musee-vicq.fr/.*

Musée d'Ennery 59 Av. Foch, 75116 Paris. The Musée d'Ennery is a national museum of Asian art located in the 16th arrondissement of Paris at 59, avenue Foch, Paris, France. The museum has grown from a private collection first begun in the second half of the 19th century by Clémence d'Ennery, wife of playwright Adolphe Philippe d'Ennery. *Website: guimet.fr/fr/musee-d-ennery.*

Musée d'Histoire Contemporaine 184 Cr Nicole Dreyfus, 92000 Nanterre, France La contemporaine is a French library, museum and archive center specialized on 20th century history. It was named "Bibliothèque de documentation internationale contemporaine" in 2018. The institution has two centers, one on the Paris Nanterre University campus, which hosts the archives and the library. *Website: lacontemporaine.fr/collections/quels-documents.*

Musée d'Histoire de la Médecine 12 rue de l'École de Médecine, 75006 Paris. The headquarters of Paris Cité University, located in the premises of the former Faculty of Medicine, offers the general public the opportunity to discover its Museum of the History of Medicine. Full price is €3.50. *Website: u-paris.fr/musee-de-lhistoire-de-la-medecine.*

Musée d'Orsay Esplanade Valéry Giscard d'Estaing, 75007 Paris. The Musée d'Orsay is a Paris museum on the Left Bank of the Seine. It is housed in the former Gare d'Orsay, a Beaux-Arts railway station built between 1898 and 1900. The museum holds mainly French art from 1848 to 1914, including paintings, sculptures, furniture, and photography. *Website: musee-orsay.fr.*

Musée de l'Armée 129 rue de Grenelle, 75007 Paris. The Musée de l'Armée is a national military museum of France located at Les Invalides in the 7th arrondissement of Paris. It is served by Paris Métro stations Invalides, Varenne and La Tour-Maubourg. The Musée de l'Armée was created in 1905 with the merger of the Musée d'Artillerie and the Musée Historique de l'Armée. *Website: musee-armee.fr/ac-cueil.html.*

Musée de l'Éventail 2 boulevard de Strasbourg, Paris. The Musée de l'Éventail, or more formally L'Atelier Hoguet Musée de l'Éventail, is a private museum of fans and fan-making located in the 10th arrondissement. *Website: amis-musee-eventails.com/le-musee/.*

Musée des Archives Nationales 60 rue des Francs-Bourgeois, 75003 Paris. Exhibit of documents drawn from the Archives Nationales. *Website: archives-nationales.culture.gouv.fr.*

Musée de l'Homme 17 Pl. du Trocadéro et du 11 Novembre, 75116 Paris. The Musée de l'Homme is an anthropology museum in Paris, France. It was established in 1937 by Paul Rivet for the 1937 Exposition Internationale des Arts et Techniques dans la Vie Moderne. It is the descendant of the Musée d'Ethnographie du Trocadéro, founded in 1878. It is one of the two musumes at the Trocadero. *Website: museedelhomme.fr.*

Musée de l'Orangerie Jardin des Tuileries, 75001 Paris. The Musée de l'Orangerie is an art gallery of impressionist and post-impressionist paintings located in the west corner of the Tuileries Garden next to the Place de la Concorde in Paris. It is home to *The Water Lilies* by Claude Monet. *Website: musee-orangerie.fr.*

Musée de l'Ordre de la Libération 129 rue de Grenelle, 75007 Paris. Located in the Hôtel national des Invalides, history of the Free French Forces in World War II. *Website: ordredelaliberation.fr.*

Musée de la Chasse et de la Nature 62 rue des Archives, 75003 Paris. The Musée de la Chasse et de la Nature is a private museum of hunting and nature located in the 3rd arrondissement. The Rambuteau Paris Métro station serves the museum. Exhibits focus on the relationships between humans and the natural environment through the traditions and practices of hunting. *Website: chassenature.org.*

Musée de la Contrefaçon 16 rue de la Faisanderie, 75116 Paris. The Musée de la Contrefaçon is a museum of counterfeiting. It is located in the 16th arrondissement and is open daily except Monday. This museum is run by The Museum of the Union of Manufacturers and is about fake products. The nearest métro and RER stations are Porte Dauphine and Avenue Foch. *Website: musee-contrefacon.com.*

Musée de la Franc-Maçonnerie 16 rue Cadet, 75009 Paris The Musée de la Franc-Maçonnerie is a museum of Freemasonry located in the 9th arrondissement at 16, rue Cadet, Paris, France. It is open daily except Sundays and Mondays; an admission fee is charged. The closest metro station is Cadet. *Website: museefm.org/.*

Musée de la Magie 11 rue Saint-Paul, 75004 Paris. The Musée de la Magie, also known as the Musée de la Curiosité et de la Magie and the Académie de la Magie, is a private museum. It is open several afternoons per week. *Website: museedelamagie.com.*

Musée de la Cinémathèque 51 rue de Bercy, 75012 Paris. Well-known organization in a Frank Gehry–designed building with a museum & film screenings. *Website: cinematheque.fr.*

Monnaie de Paris 11 Quai de Conti, 75006 Paris. The Monnaie de Paris is a government-owned institution responsible for producing France's coins. Founded in AD 864 with the Edict of Pistres, it is the world's oldest continuously running minting institution. *Website: monnaiedeparis.fr.*

Musée de la Musique 221 Av. Jean Jaurès, 75019 Paris. The Musée de la Musique de la Philharmonie de Paris is a French museum in Paris, inaugurated in 1997. *Website: philharmoniedeparis.fr/fr.*

Musée de La Poste 34 Bd de Vaugirard, 75015 Paris. The Musée de La Poste is the museum of the French postal operator La Poste. It specializes in the postal history and philately of France. Opened in 1946, the museum has been located on two sites in Paris. *Website: museedelaposte.fr/fr.*

Musée de la Sculpture en Plein Air 11 Bis Quai Saint-Bernard, 75005 Paris. The Musée de la Sculpture en Plein Air is a collection of outdoor sculptures on the Seine banks. The outdoor space was created in 1980 in the Jardin Tino Rossi to display sculptures from the second half of the twentieth century. *Wikipedia: https://en.wikipedia.org/wiki/Mus%C3%A9e_de_la_Sculpture_en_Plein_Air.*

Musée de la Vie Romantique 16 rue Chaptal, 75009 Paris. The Musée de la Vie Romantique is one of three literary museums in Paris. It is located at the foot of Montmartre. There is a bakery and tea room. *Website: museevieromantique.paris.fr/en.*

Musée de Minéralogie de l'école des Mines 60 Bd Saint-Michel, 75006 Paris. The Musée de Minéralogie is a museum of mineralogy operated by the École nationale supérieure des mines de Paris. It is located inside the building of Mines Paris. It is open daily except Sunday and Monday; Minerals, artificial minerals, rocks, ores, and gems. *Website: musee.minesparis.psl.eu/Accueil/.*

Musée de Montmartre 12 rue Cortot, 75018 Paris. Art museum tracing local history & culture, in 17th-century house & garden where Renoir once worked. *Website: museedemontmartre.fr/.*

Musée des Arts Décoratifs MAD PARIS, 107 rue de Rivoli, 75001 Paris. Les Arts Décoratifs is a private, non-profit organization that manages decorative arts museums. The first museum dates to 1882, when collectors interested in the applied arts formed the initial organization. *Website: madparis.fr.*

Musée des Arts et Métiers 292 rue Saint-Martin, 75141 Paris The Musée des Arts et Métiers is an industrial design museum in Paris that houses the collection of the Conservatoire National des Arts et Métiers, which was founded in 1794 as a repository for the preservation of scientific instruments and inventions. *Website: arts-et-metiers.net.*

Les Pavillons de Bercy - Musée des Arts Forains 53 Av. des Terroirs de France, 75012 Paris. Funfair objects include amusement rides, fair stalls, restored attractions, merry-go-rounds and carousels, and German swings. Located within the Pavillons de Bercy. It is open to the public by prior reservation. Guided tours are available on a limited basis, and admission may be booked via their website. *Website: arts-forains.com/en/visitors/individual-visitor.*

Musée des Collections Historiques de la Préfecture de Police 4 rue de la Montagne Ste Geneviève, 75005 Paris Located in the police headquarters in the 5th and 6th arrondissements, the museum traces the history of the Parisian police from the 17th century to the present day through the presentation of more than 2,000 original and diverse works. *Website: prefecturedepolice.interieur.gouv.fr/musee.*

Musée des Égouts de Paris, Paris Sewer Museum Esplanade Habib Bourguiba, Pont de l'Alma, 75007 Paris. History of tours of the Paris sewer system, role of sewer workers, and water treatment methods. Tickets are just under 10 euros, but check the website for guided tours and workshops. *Website: musee-egouts.paris.fr.*

Musée des Moulages Dermatologiques de l'hôpital Saint-Louis, 1 Av. Claude Vellefaux, 75010 Paris. With its five thousand casts, the Museum nestled in the heart of the historic buildings of the Saint-Louis hospital, is a unique place in both Paris and the world. Website: hopital-saintlouis.aphp.fr/le-musee-des-moulages-de-lhopital-de-saint-louis/.

Musée des Plans-Reliefs Hôtel national des Invalides, 129, rue de Grenelle, 75007 Paris. Relief maps were invented in the 17th century when Louvois, Louis XIV's Minister of War, commissioned Vauban to make a scale model of the city of Dunkirk. The Museum, now run by the Ministry of Culture and located within the Hôtel des Invalides, offers 28 examples of a collection of relief maps of fortified towns made between 1668 and 1875. *Website: musee-armee.fr/en/ your-visit/museum-spaces/musee-des-plans-reliefs.html.*

Musée du Barreau de Paris 25 rue du Jour, 75001 Paris. History of the Paris Bar and its lawyers. Check the website for tickets and visit details. At the time of this writing, the museum website says it is closed indefinitely. *Website: museedubarreaudeparis.com.*

Musée du Fumeur 7 rue Pache 75011 Paris, Includes smoking pipes, Egyptian sheeshas, snuffboxes, cigars, tobacco samples, hemp-fiber clothing, etchings, portraits, photographs, videos, and scientific drawings of tobacco plants.

There is also an extensive online store. *Website: museedu-fumeur.net.*

Musée du Louvre 75001 Paris. The Louvre is a national art museum in Paris, France. It is located on the Right Bank of the Seine in the city's 1st arrondissement and home to some of the most canonical works of Western art, including the Mona Lisa and the Venus de Milo. *Website: louvre.fr/en/visit.*

Musée du Général Leclerc de Hauteclocque et de la Libération de Paris – Musée Jean Moulin 4 Avenue du Colonel Henri Rol-Tanguay, 75014 Paris. Maréchal Philippe Leclerc de Hauteclocque, Jean Moulin, a major figure of the French Resistance and the liberation of Paris in World War II. *Website: museeliberation-leclerc-moulin.paris.fr.*

Musée du Luxembourg 19 rue de Vaugirard, 75006 Paris. The museum hosts two annual exhibitions, focusing on 20th-century painting, photography & women artists. 6th Art Changing Exhibitions of art. *Website: museeduluxembourg.fr.*

Musée du Parfum Fragonard 9 rue Scribe, 75009 Paris. A French private museum of perfume history and process of perfume, antique perfume bottles, containers, toiletry sets, and 19th-century period rooms. *Website: musee-parfum-paris.fragonard.com.*

Musée du quai Branly - Jacques Chirac, 37 Quai Jacques Chirac, 75007 Paris. Indigenous art and cultures of Africa, Asia, Oceania, and the Americas. *Website: quaibranly.fr.*

Musée du Service de Santé des Armées Museum of the Armed Forces Health Services,1 Pl. Alphonse Laveran, 75005 Paris 5th Medical History of medical care for armed services in France. The Army Health Service (SSA) museum, installed in the cloister of the former royal abbey of Val-de-Grâce, offers visitors a panorama of military medicine. *Website: defense.gouv.fr/sante/musee-du-service-sante-armees.*

Musée du Vin 5 Square Charles Dickens - 75016 Paris History of the French craft of winemaking includes tools and objects used to work the grapevine and the wine, a wine cellar, and cooperage. It is private, small, and commercial. *Website: lemparis.com.*

Musée en Herbe The Grass Museum. 23 rue de l'Arbre Sec, 75001 Paris. Art museum for children. *Website: museeen-herbe.com.*

Musée Grévin 10 Bd Montmartre, 75009 Paris The Musée Grévin is a wax museum located on the Grands Boulevards in the 9th arrondissement of Paris on the right bank of the Seine. *Website: grevin-paris.com.*

Musée Jacquemart-André 158 Bd Haussmann, 75008 Paris. The Musée Jacquemart-André is a private museum located at 158 Boulevard Haussmann in the 8th arrondissement of Paris. The museum was created from the private home of Édouard André and Nélie Jacquemart to display the art they collected during their lives. Currently under renovation, planned opening September 2024. *Website: musee-jacquemart-andre.com.*

Musée Maillol 59-61 rue de Grenelle, 75007 Paris. Works by Aristide Maillol and art exhibitions. *Website: museemaillol.com.*

Musée Marmottan Monet 2 rue Louis Boilly, 75016 Paris. Dedicated to artist Claude Monet. The collection features over three hundred Impressionist and Post-Impressionist paintings by Claude Monet, including his 1872 Impression, *Sunrise.* website: marmottan.fr

Musée National d'Art Moderne Place Georges-Pompidou, 75004 Paris. With about 15,000 works, The City of Paris Museum of Modern Art Museum collections represent the wealth of the artistic creation in the 20th and 21st centuries and testify to the dynamism of the contemporary artistic scene. *Website: mam.paris.fr/en.*

Musée national de la Légion d'Honneur et des Ordres de Chevalerie 2 rue de la Légion d'Honneur, 75007 Paris. The National Museum of the Legion of Honor and Orders of Chivalry is a French national museum of orders of merit and orders of chivalry. It is located in the Palais de la Légion d'Honneur beside the Musée d'Orsay. *Website: legiondhonneur.fr/fr/page/le-musee-de-la-legion-dhonneur-et-des-ordres-de-chevalerie/249.*

Musée National de la Marine Palais de Chaillot 17 place du Trocadéro 75016 Paris. Maritime Includes ship models, maritime art, artifacts, and photos. *Website: musee-marine.fr.*

Musée National des Arts Asiatiques-Guimet 6 Pl. d'Iéna, 75116 Paris. The museum has one of the largest collections of Asian art outside of Asia. *Website: guimet.fr.*

Musée de Cluny - Musée National du Moyen Âge 28 rue du Sommerard, 75005 Paris The Lady and the Unicorn tapestries, remnants of the third century Gallo-Roman baths, mostly middle ages artwork with intriguing exhibits. *Website: musee-moyenage.fr.*

Musée National Eugène Delacroix 6 rue de Furstemberg, 75006 Paris. Art, life, and works of Eugène Delacroix. Re-opening March 2024. *Website: musee-delacroix.fr.*

Musée National Gustave Moreau 14 rue Catherine de la Rochefoucauld, 75009 Paris. The Musée National Gustave Moreau (1826-1898) is an art museum dedicated to the works of Symbolist painter. *Website: musee-moreau.fr.*

Musée National Jean-Jacques Henner 43 Av. de Villiers, 75017 Paris. Art House and works of painter Jean-Jacques Henner (1829–1905). *Website: musee-henner.fr.*

Musée Nissim de Camondo 63 rue de Monceau, 75008 Paris. The Musée Nissim de Camondo is a historic house museum of French decorative arts located in the Hôtel Moïse de Camondo. It is beautifully well-preserved and has a restaurant. This is part of the MAD, MUSÉE DES ARTS DÉCORATIFS. *Website: madparis.fr/Musee-Nissim-de-Camondo-742.*

Musée Pasteur 25 rue du Dr Roux, 75015 Paris. The life of scientist Louis Pasteur Museum is currently under long-term refurbishment. Check the website for updates. *Website: pasteur.fr/en/institut-pasteur/museum.*

Musée Picasso 5 rue de Thorigny, 75003 Paris. Art Life and work of artist Pablo Picasso, also works by Cézanne, Degas, Rousseau, Seurat, de Chirico and Matisse, Iberian bronzes, African art. *Website: museepicassoparis.fr.*

Musée Pierre Cardin 93400 Saint-Ouen-sur-Seine. Over 250 Haute Couture designs from 1950 to 2000 designed by Pierre Cardin. This museum is closed with no plan for reopening, but check their website for updates if you're interested in visiting. *Website: pierrecardin.com/museum.*

Musée Rodin 77 rue de Varenne, 75007 Paris. Works of the French sculptors Auguste Rodin and Camille Claudel, located in the Hôtel Biron. *Website: musee-rodin.fr.*

Musée Yves Saint Laurent Paris 5 Av. Marceau, 75116 Paris. Operated by the Fondation Pierre Bergé – Yves Saint Laurent works by the fashion designer Yves Saint Laurent. Check the website for details. *Website: museeyslparis.com.*

Musée Zadkine 100 bis rue d'Assas, 75006 Paris. The Musée Zadkine is a workshop and museum dedicated to the work of Russian sculptor Ossip Zadkine. It is located near the Jardin du Luxembourg. *Website: zadkine.paris.fr.*

Muséum National d'Histoire Naturelle 57 rue Cuvier 75005 Paris. The Natural History Museum includes galleries for minerals and gems, fossils and dinosaurs, comparative anatomy, and the Grand Gallery of Evolution. *Website: www.mnhn.fr.*

Palais de la Découverte 186 rue Saint Charles 75015 Paris. Includes interactive exhibits for mathematics, physics, astronomy, chemistry, geology, and biology. *Website: palais-decouverte.fr.*

Palais de Tokyo 13 Av. du Président Wilson, 75116 Paris. Modern and contemporary art. *Website: palaisdetokyo.com.*

Palais Galliera 10 Av. Pierre 1er de Serbie, 75116 Paris. Also known as Musée de la Mode et du Costume de la Ville de Paris, fashion and fashion history includes exhibits of French fashion design and costume from the eighteenth century to the present, closed between exhibitions. *Website: palaisgalliera.paris.fr.*

Pavillon de l'Arsenal 21 Bd Morland, 75004 Paris. Architecture and urban planning. *Website: pavillon-arsenal.com.*

Pavillon de l'Eau 77 Av. de Versailles, 75016 Paris. History of the city's water supply. The pavilion is closed, but may reopen at some point. *Website: eaudeparis.fr/le-pavillon-de-leau.*

Petit Palais Avenue Winston-Churchill, 75008 Paris. Paintings, sculpture, Ancient Greek and Roman art, Renaissance art, and art 17th, 18th, and 19th-century art. *Website: petitpalais.paris.fr.*

Tour Jean-sans-Peur 20 rue Étienne Marcel 75002 Paris. History of the medieval tower and medieval Paris. It was the home OF The grand Parisian Palace of the Duke of Burgundy. *Website: tourjeansanspeursite.wordpress.com.*

Chapter 13

Shopping on the Champs-Élysées

The Champs-Élysées is one of the most famous streets in Paris and the world. It is located in the 8th arrondissement of Paris and runs from the Place de la Concorde to the Arc de Triomphe. The street is known for its high-end shops, cafes, and theaters, and is a popular tourist destination.

The history of the Champs-Élysées dates back to the 17th century when it was originally a tree-lined pathway. In the 18th century, it was extended and became a fashionable promenade for the French aristocracy. It was also the site of some of the most significant events in French history, including the storming of the Tuileries Palace during the French Revolution.

In the early 19th century, the Champs-Élysées underwent a significant transformation, with the addition of new buildings and public spaces. The Arc de Triomphe was built at the western end of the street in 1806 to commemorate the victories of Napoleon Bonaparte. The Place de la Concorde, located at the eastern end of the Champs-Élysées, was also redesigned during this time.

In the 20th century, the Champs-Élysées became a symbol of French cultural and economic prosperity. It was the site of numerous parades and celebrations, including the annual Bastille Day military parade. During World War II, the Champs-Élysées was occupied by German forces and was the site of several important battles.

In the post-war period, the Champs-Élysées underwent significant changes. The street became known for its high-end luxury shops and restaurants, and it was increasingly targeted toward tourists. In 1975, the Champs-Élysées was pedestrianized on Sundays, allowing visitors to enjoy the street without the noise and pollution of cars.

Today, the Champs-Élysées is one of the most famous and visited streets in the world. It attracts millions of tourists every year, who come to see its shops, cafes, and famous landmarks. Despite its commercialization, the Champs-Élysées remains an important symbol of French culture and history. It is a testament to the city's rich and diverse past and a reminder of its continued importance in the modern world.

Chapter 14

Wonderful Places
to go in Paris

Paris is a city that boasts an abundance of paid museums and attractions that visitors can explore to their heart's content. There's something for everyone in this cultural capital, and if you're looking to take full advantage of all the city has to offer, then the Paris Museum Pass might just be the perfect option for you.

The Paris Museum Pass is an excellent way to make the most of your time in Paris while keeping your expenses under control. With the pass, you can gain one-time access to all the attractions listed on it. You can purchase the pass for up to 6 days, giving you ample time to explore the city's incredible museums and landmarks.

For example, during our recent trip to Paris, my family and I used the Paris Museum Pass for 4 days, which cost us 70 euros each. With this pass, we were granted admission to some of the city's most famous landmarks, such as the Museum of the Art and History of Judaism, the Arc de

Triomphe, the Louvre, Versailles, and the Musee d'Orsay. The total cost of admission for all these attractions was a whopping 76 euros, so the pass was definitely worth it in terms of cost savings.

It's essential to note that the Paris Museum Pass works in days and hours. The passes must be used within the time allotted and can be only used for a single admission. Visitors have a choice of three passes: 2 days [48 h], 4 days [96 h], or 6 days [144 h].

Most museums in Paris have time reservation requirements that must be observed. However, by purchasing your tickets ahead of time or using the Paris Museum Pass, you won't have to worry about getting disappointed at the door. For this itinerary, we found it easier to use the pass and make unpaid reservations at all the venues.

Although the Paris Museum Pass offers great value for money, it's essential to plan ahead to make the most of it. During our visit, we had planned on going to an additional museum. However, my daughter had her heart set on visiting the catacombs on Friday and wanted to skip Musée de l'Orangerie on Friday afternoon. Had we gone to Musée de l'Orangerie, it would have made for exceptional value.

So, if you're looking to make the most of your time in Paris and explore its incredible cultural offerings, the Paris Museum Pass is definitely worth considering. With so many museums and landmarks to explore, the pass will allow you to experience all that Paris has to offer without breaking the bank. Just be sure to plan ahead, make your reservations, and use the pass within the allotted time frame.

The Louvre

The Louvre is one of the world's most famous and iconic museums, located in the heart of Paris, France. The museum is home to over 38,000 works of art, ranging from ancient artifacts to contemporary masterpieces, and attracts millions of visitors every year.

The Louvre was originally built as a fortress in the late 12th century under King Philip II, and was later converted into a royal palace during the 16th century. In 1793, the palace was opened as a public museum, and has since become one of the most visited and celebrated cultural institutions in the world.

The Louvre's collection is vast and varied, spanning many different cultures, time periods, and artistic styles. Some of the museum's most famous works include the *Mona Lisa*, the *Winged Victory of Samothrace*, and the *Venus de Milo*. The Louvre also has an extensive collection of Egyptian antiquities.

In addition to its permanent collection, the Louvre also hosts a number of temporary exhibitions throughout the year. These exhibitions often focus on a specific artist or time period, and provide visitors with a deeper understanding of the artworks and their historical context.

One of the most impressive features of the Louvre is its architecture. The museum is housed in a sprawling complex of buildings, including the iconic Louvre Pyramid, designed by architect I.M. Pei in 1989. The pyramid serves as the main entrance to the museum and has become an emblem of the Louvre's grandeur and prestige.

Visiting the Louvre can be an overwhelming experience, given the size and scope of its collection. However, the museum offers a number of resources and services to help visitors navigate its galleries and appreciate its artworks. Audio guides are available in multiple languages, and the Louvre also offers guided tours and workshops for visitors of all ages.

Overall, the Louvre is a must-see destination for anyone interested in art, culture, and history. Its vast collection and stunning architecture make it one of the world's most unique and inspiring museums, and a testament to the enduring power and beauty of human creativity.

The Louvre is one of the world's largest and most famous museums, and there is no shortage of incredible artworks and artifacts to see. It can be overwhelming to decide where to start, so here are the top five things to see at the Louvre:

1. The *Mona Lisa* by Leonardo da Vinci: This is perhaps the most famous painting in the world, and it is the star attraction of the Louvre. Visitors will likely encounter large crowds gathered around this small portrait, which is housed in its own dedicated room. Despite the crowds, the painting's enigmatic smile and technical mastery make it a must-see for any art lover.

2. The *Winged Victory of Samothrace*: This stunning marble statue of the Greek goddess Nike is considered one of the finest examples of Hellenistic sculpture. The statue's dynamic pose and flowing drapery make it seem as though it is caught in motion, and its dramatic setting atop a staircase in the Daru staircase emphasizes its grandeur.

3. The *Venus de Milo*: This ancient Greek statue of the goddess Aphrodite (known as Venus in Roman

mythology) is another highlight of the Louvre's collection. The statue's graceful form and delicate features have made it a symbol of classical beauty, and it is one of the most iconic artworks of the ancient world.

4. Egyptian Antiquities: The Louvre has an extensive collection of Egyptian art and artifacts, including the Seated Scribe. These objects provide a fascinating glimpse into the culture and beliefs of one of the world's most ancient civilizations, and the Louvre's collection is one of the best outside of Egypt itself.

5. The Napoleon III Apartments: These opulent apartments were once used by Emperor Napoleon III and his wife, Empress Eugénie as their private residence within the Louvre. The rooms are lavishly decorated with gilded furniture, paintings, and sculptures and provide a glimpse into the luxurious lifestyle of French royalty during the 19th century.

These are just a few of the many incredible artworks and artifacts to see at the Louvre. Visitors can easily spend an entire day exploring the museum's galleries and discovering hidden treasures, and the Louvre is a must-see destination for anyone interested in art, culture, and history.

The Museum of the Art and History of Judaism

The Museum of the Art and History of Judaism, located in the Marais district of Paris, is a unique cultural institution showcasing Jewish culture's rich history and traditions. The museum is housed in a historic building that was once the Hôtel de Saint-Aignan, and its collection includes over

12,000 works of art, artifacts, and documents related to Jewish life and culture.

The museum's permanent collection is organized around several themes, including Jewish ceremonial art, Jewish history and traditions, and Jewish life in France. Highlights of the collection include a stunning collection of Torah mantles, ornate coverings for Torah scrolls, and a collection of Hanukkah lamps from around the world. Visitors can also see a collection of Jewish wedding rings, which provide a fascinating glimpse into the traditions and customs surrounding Jewish marriage.

The museum also has a collection of works by modern and contemporary Jewish artists, including Marc Chagall and Chaim Soutine. These artworks provide a unique perspective on Jewish life and culture in the 20th and 21st centuries and demonstrate the ongoing relevance and vitality of Jewish artistic traditions.

In addition to its permanent collection, the Museum of the Art and History of Judaism also hosts temporary exhibitions throughout the year. These exhibitions often explore specific themes related to Jewish history and culture, and provide visitors with a deeper understanding of the many facets of Jewish life and traditions.

One of the most impressive features of the museum is its historic building. The Hôtel de Saint-Aignan was originally built in the 17th century for a wealthy nobleman, and has been carefully restored to its original grandeur. The building's architecture is a fascinating blend of French and Jewish styles, and includes stunning examples of Baroque and Rococo design.

Visiting the Museum of the Art and History of Judaism is a unique and rewarding experience for anyone interested in

Jewish culture and history. The museum's collection is vast and varied, and provides a comprehensive look at the many traditions and customs of Jewish life.

The Museum of Art and History of Judaism in Paris is home to an impressive collection of over 12,000 objects that illustrate the rich and diverse history and culture of Jewish life. Here are the top five things to see at the museum:

1. Torah mantles: The museum boasts an extensive collection of Torah mantles, ornate coverings for Torah scrolls. These richly embroidered and decorated textiles provide insight into the artistic traditions of Jewish communities throughout the world.

2. Hanukkah lamps: The museum's collection of Hanukkah lamps features examples from around the world, including Europe, North Africa, and the Middle East. These lamps, used during the eight-day Jewish festival of Hanukkah, demonstrate the many artistic styles and cultural influences that have shaped Jewish art and tradition.

3. Jewish wedding rings: The museum's collection of Jewish wedding rings showcases the wide variety of styles and materials used in traditional Jewish wedding ceremonies. From simple gold bands to intricate diamond-encrusted designs, these rings provide a glimpse into the rituals and customs surrounding Jewish marriage.

4. Marc Chagall's stained glass windows: The museum houses a set of stunning stained glass windows designed by the renowned Jewish artist Marc Chagall. The windows were created for the synagogue of the

Hadassah Medical Center in Jerusalem and were donated to the museum in 1962.

5. Contemporary art exhibitions: The museum regularly hosts temporary exhibitions of contemporary art by Jewish artists from around the world. These exhibitions provide a platform for artists to explore and express their Jewish identity and heritage, and offer visitors a glimpse into the ongoing evolution of Jewish art and culture.

Overall, the Museum of Art and History of Judaism is a must-see destination for anyone interested in Jewish history and culture. Its extensive collection of art and artifacts, combined with its dynamic exhibitions and stunning architecture, make it a fascinating and rewarding cultural experience.

The Jewish Quarter

The Jewish Quarter in Paris, also known as the Pletzl, is located in the heart of the city's Marais district. The history of the Jewish community in Paris can be traced back to the Middle Ages, when Jews began settling in the area. Over the years, the Jewish Quarter has undergone many changes, but it remains a vibrant and thriving community to this day.

One of the most notable features of the Jewish Quarter is the Rue des Rosiers, a street that is lined with kosher restaurants, bakeries, and shops. This street has become synonymous with the Jewish community in Paris and is a popular destination for both locals and tourists.

The Jewish Quarter is also home to several historic synagogues, including the Synagogue de la Victoire, which was built in the 1870s and is one of the largest synagogues in Paris. The synagogue's stunning architecture, with its impressive dome and stained glass windows, is a testament to the community's resilience and determination to maintain their cultural identity.

Another important site in the Jewish Quarter is the Shoah Memorial, which is dedicated to the memory of the Jewish victims of the Holocaust. The museum features exhibits on the history of the Holocaust, as well as the experiences of Jews in France during this time. The Shoah Memorial serves as a reminder of the atrocities committed against the Jewish people and the importance of educating future generations about the dangers of hatred and prejudice.

In addition to its rich cultural heritage, the Jewish Quarter is also a hub for contemporary Jewish culture. The Marais district is home to several Jewish cultural institutions, including the Centre Medem Arbeter Ring, which hosts concerts, lectures, and other events celebrating Jewish culture.

The Jewish Quarter has also played an important role in shaping the broader cultural landscape of Paris. The community's presence has contributed to the city's vibrant artistic and intellectual traditions, with many notable Jewish artists, writers, and thinkers making their mark on Parisian culture.

Despite its rich history and cultural significance, the Jewish Quarter has not been immune to the challenges facing Jewish communities around the world. In recent years, there has been a rise in anti-Semitic incidents in France, and the Jewish community in the Marais has not been spared. Despite these challenges, however, the community has remained resilient and committed to preserving its traditions and cultural identity.

In conclusion, the Jewish Quarter in Paris is a rich and vibrant community that has played an important role in the city's cultural and intellectual history. From its historic synagogues to its bustling kosher restaurants, the Pletzl remains a thriving cultural hub that celebrates the community's past, present, and future. While the challenges facing the community are real and significant, the Jewish Quarter serves as a reminder of the importance of preserving cultural heritage and standing up against hatred and prejudice.

The Palace of Versailles

The Palace of Versailles, located just outside of Paris, is one of the most famous and opulent royal residences in the world. Originally built as a hunting lodge for Louis XIII in 1623, the palace was transformed into a grandiose symbol of the power and wealth of the French monarchy by Louis XIV in the late 17th century.

Today, the Palace of Versailles is a UNESCO World Heritage site and one of the most popular tourist attractions in France. Visitors can explore the palace's ornate halls, grand staircases, and opulent apartments, as well as its extensive gardens and fountains.

The palace's most famous feature is undoubtedly the Hall of Mirrors. This grandiose gallery, which stretches over 230 feet and features 17 mirrored arches, was designed by Louis XIV's chief architect, Jules Hardouin-Mansart, in the late 17th century. The hall was used for court ceremonies and balls, and served as a grand showcase of the power and splendor of the French monarchy.

Other highlights of the palace include the King's and Queen's State Apartments, which are decorated with elaborate frescoes, tapestries, and gilded furniture. The apartments were designed to impress and intimidate visitors with their grandeur and opulence, and provide a fascinating glimpse into the world of the French aristocracy in the 17th and 18th centuries.

Visitors to the Palace of Versailles can also explore the palace's extensive gardens, which cover over 800 hectares and include formal parterres, groves, and fountains. The gardens are dotted with sculptures and pavilions, and offer stunning views of the palace and its surrounding landscape.

One of the most impressive features of the gardens is the Grand Canal, a massive waterway that stretches over 5 kilometers in length. Visitors can rent rowboats or take a leisurely stroll along the canal, enjoying the serene beauty of the water and the surrounding greenery.

Another highlight of the gardens is the Fountain Show, a spectacular display of water and music that takes place during the summer months. The show features synchronized water jets, classical music, and colorful lighting effects, and is a must-see for anyone visiting the Palace of Versailles.

In summary, the Palace of Versailles is a magnificent symbol of the wealth and power of the French monarchy, and a testament to the artistry and craftsmanship of the greatest architects, artists, and designers of the 17th and 18th centuries. Its grandeur, opulence, and historical significance make it a must-see destination for anyone visiting France.

The Palace of Versailles is a grandiose royal residence that has been a symbol of the power and wealth of the French monarchy for centuries. Here are the top five things to see when visiting the Palace of Versailles:

1. The Hall of Mirrors: This grand gallery, which features 17 mirrored arches, is one of the most famous rooms in the palace. It was designed by Jules Hardouin-Mansart in the late 17th century and served as a showcase for the French monarchy's grandeur and wealth.
2. The King's State Apartments: These apartments, which include the King's Bedchamber and the Salon of Hercules, are decorated with ornate frescoes, tapestries, and gilded furniture.
3. The Queen's State Apartments: The Queen's State Apartments, which include the Queen's Bedchamber and the Salon of Venus, are just as grand and opulent as the King's. They are decorated with beautiful paintings, sculptures, and tapestries that reflect the luxurious taste of the French queens.
4. The Gardens: The Palace of Versailles is surrounded by extensive gardens that cover over 800 hectares. The gardens feature formal parterres, groves, and fountains, as well as sculptures and pavilions. They offer a serene escape from the palace's grandeur and are a great place to relax and enjoy nature.
5. The Grand Trianon: The Grand Trianon is a separate palace that was built by Louis XIV as a retreat from the main palace. It features beautiful gardens and a unique architectural style that blends classical and Asian influences. It offers a fascinating glimpse into the personal life of the French kings and queens.

Overall, the Palace of Versailles is a must-see destination for anyone visiting France. Its grandeur, opulence, and historical significance make it one of the most impressive and awe-inspiring attractions in the world.

Arc de Triomphe

The Arc de Triomphe is one of the most iconic landmarks in Paris, standing at the center of the Place Charles de Gaulle and towering over the surrounding streets. This impressive monument was commissioned by Napoleon Bonaparte in 1806 to celebrate his military victories, but it was not completed until 1836, after his death.

The Arc de Triomphe is designed in the neoclassical style and features intricate carvings and sculptures that depict various scenes from French history. The most famous of these is the Relief of the Departure of the Volunteers of 1792, also known as La Marseillaise. This stunning sculpture depicts a group of soldiers and civilians marching off to fight for the French Revolution, and is a powerful symbol of French patriotism and resilience.

Visitors to the Arc de Triomphe can climb to the top of the monument for a stunning panoramic view of Paris. The climb is quite steep, with 284 steps to the top, but the view is well worth the effort. From the top of the Arc de Triomphe, visitors can see the Eiffel Tower, the Champs-Élysées, and many other famous Parisian landmarks.

The Arc de Triomphe is also the site of the Tomb of the Unknown Soldier, a memorial to the many soldiers who died in World War I. The tomb is located beneath the arch and is marked by an eternal flame, which is rekindled every evening at 6:30 pm in a solemn ceremony.

One of the most popular events that takes place at the Arc de Triomphe is the annual Bastille Day military parade. This spectacular event features military bands, marching soldiers, and colorful floats, all passing through the arch to the cheers of thousands of spectators. The parade is a celebration of French national pride and a tribute to the bravery and sacrifice of the French military.

Musée d'Orsay

The Musée d'Orsay is one of the most famous art museums in the world, located in the heart of Paris. The museum is housed in a stunning Beaux-Arts building that was originally a train station, built in the late 19th century. The museum is dedicated to the art and culture of the 19th and early 20th centuries, featuring works by some of the most famous artists of the era.

One of the most famous works of art in the Musée d'Orsay is Vincent van Gogh's *Starry Night Over the Rhône*. This stunning painting depicts a night sky filled with swirling stars, reflected in the still waters of the Rhône River. The painting demonstrates to van Gogh's unique style and artistic vision, and is one of the most beloved works of art in the museum's collection.

Another famous work in the Musée d'Orsay is Edouard Manet's *Olympia*, a controversial painting that caused a scandal when it was first exhibited in 1865. The painting depicts a reclining nude woman, surrounded by a Black servant and a bouquet of flowers. The painting was seen as a challenge to traditional ideas of beauty and morality, and was a groundbreaking work of art that helped to pave the way for the modernist movement.

The Musée d'Orsay is also home to many works by the Impressionist and Post-Impressionist artists who revolutionized the art world in the late 19th century. The museum features works by Claude Monet, Pierre-Auguste Renoir, Paul Cézanne, and many others. These artists sought to capture the fleeting beauty of the natural world, using bold brushstrokes and vivid colors to create stunning works of art.

Visitors to the Musée d'Orsay can also admire the museum's stunning architecture, with its soaring ceilings, intricate metalwork, and expansive windows that flood the galleries with natural light. The museum's airy and spacious galleries provide the perfect setting for the masterpieces on display, allowing visitors to fully appreciate the beauty and complexity of the art.

The Musée d'Orsay is one of the most famous art museums in the world, with an impressive collection of works by some of the most famous artists of the 19th and early 20th centuries. Here are the top 5 things to see at the Musée d'Orsay:

1. Vincent van Gogh's *Starry Night Over the Rhône*: This stunning painting is one of the most famous works in the Musée d'Orsay's collection. Van Gogh's use of bold colors and swirling brushstrokes captures the beauty of the night sky over the Rhône River.
2. Édouard Manet's *Olympia*: This controversial painting caused a scandal when it was first exhibited in 1865. The painting depicts a reclining nude woman and challenges traditional ideas of beauty and morality.
3. Claude Monet's *Water Lilies*: The Musée d'Orsay has several works by Monet, but his *Water Lilies* series is particularly stunning. The paintings depict the serene beauty of Monet's garden at Giverny, with its water lilies, willows, and Japanese bridge.
4. Auguste Rodin's *The Kiss*: This sculpture is one of Rodin's most famous works, depicting a couple locked

in a passionate embrace. The sculpture's sensuality and emotion make it a favorite among visitors to the museum.

5. Paul Cézanne's *The Card Players*: This painting is one of Cézanne's most famous works and depicts two men engrossed in a game of cards. The painting's muted colors and simple composition highlight Cézanne's mastery of light and form.

Overall, the Musée d'Orsay has an incredible collection of works by some of the most famous artists of the 19th and early 20th centuries. These five works are just a small sample of the museum's rich and diverse collection.

Paris Catacombs

The Paris Catacombs is one of the most unique and fascinating attractions in the city, known for its eerie underground tunnels filled with bones and skulls. Located beneath the city of Paris, the catacombs have a dark and mysterious history that dates back over 200 years.

The Paris Catacombs were originally a series of limestone quarries that provided building materials for the city in the 17th and 18th centuries. Over time, the quarries grew larger and more complex, creating a vast underground network of tunnels and galleries. However, the quarries posed a danger to the city's stability and were eventually abandoned.

In the late 18th century, the city began using the abandoned quarries as a place to store human remains. With the city's cemeteries overflowing, the remains of over six million people were moved to the catacombs in a series of nighttime processions. The bones were stacked neatly in the tunnels, creating a macabre and haunting sight that can still be seen today.

Visitors to the Paris Catacombs can explore a small portion of the underground tunnels, which are open to the public. The tunnels are dimly lit and narrow, creating a sense of claustrophobia and unease. The walls are lined with skulls and bones, arranged in elaborate patterns and designs.

The catacombs also contain several areas of historical significance. One such area is the Crypt of the Sepulchral Lamp, a chamber filled with ornate carvings and a large stone altar. Another is the ossuary of the Port-Mahon gallery, where visitors can see the remains of prisoners who died in a Spanish prison camp during the 18th century.

In addition to their historical significance, the Paris Catacombs have also inspired countless works of literature and art. The catacombs have been featured in films such as *As Above, So Below* and *The Phantom of the Opera*. They have also been the subject of numerous books, poems, and songs.

While the Paris Catacombs may be a haunting and eerie attraction, they also offer a unique glimpse into the history and culture of the city. Visitors to the catacombs can learn about the city's past and explore a fascinating underground world that few have seen.

Seine Cruise

A Bateaux Parisians Seine Cruise is an excellent way to explore the city of Paris from a unique perspective. The cruise takes you along the River Seine, which winds its way through the heart of the city, offering stunning views of some of Paris's most famous landmarks and attractions.

The Bateaux Parisians Seine Cruise is an experience that allows you to see Paris from a different angle, giving you the opportunity to appreciate the city's beauty in a new light. The boats are spacious, comfortable and provide a relaxed and comfortable way to enjoy the stunning scenery that Paris has to offer.

One of the highlights of the Bateaux Parisians Seine Cruise is the opportunity to see the Eiffel Tower from the river. The Tower is visible from many parts of the city, but it is a truly breathtaking sight when seen from the Seine. The boat will take you right up close to the Tower, giving you a unique and unforgettable view of this iconic landmark.

The cruise also takes you past many other famous landmarks and attractions in the city. You'll see the Louvre Museum, the Musée d'Orsay, the Notre-Dame Cathedral, and many other sights that make Paris one of the most beautiful cities in the world. The boat travels slowly, so there is plenty of time to take in the views and snap photos of these incredible sights.

One of the great things about the Bateaux Parisians Seine Cruise is that it is suitable for people of all ages. Whether you are traveling with young children or are a seasoned traveler, this is an experience that can be enjoyed by all. The boats are spacious and comfortable, and the staff is friendly and knowledgeable, providing interesting commentary throughout the journey.

Another great feature of the Bateaux Parisians Seine Cruise is the option to enjoy a meal onboard. The boats have an excellent restaurant where you can savor delicious French cuisine while taking in the stunning views of the city. The meals are prepared using fresh, seasonal ingredients and are accompanied by a selection of fine wines.

Overall, the Bateaux Parisians Seine Cruise is an excellent way to experience the beauty and magic of Paris. The cruise takes you past some of the city's most famous landmarks and attractions, giving you a unique perspective on this magnificent city. Whether you're visiting Paris for the first time or are a seasoned traveler, a Seine Cruise is an experience that you won't want to miss.

Trocadero Gardens

The Trocadero Gardens are another popular attraction, and they offer stunning views of the Eiffel Tower. The gardens are beautifully landscaped and are a great place to relax and enjoy the scenery. Visitors can also enjoy a picnic in the gardens while taking in the breathtaking views of the Eiffel Tower.

The Trocadero also has a large fountain, the Fontaine de Varsovie, which is located at the center of the gardens. The fountain is an impressive sight, and its design is inspired by the fountains found in the Palace of Versailles. The fountain is illuminated at night, creating a stunning visual display that is not to be missed.

One of the unique features of the Trocadero is its historical significance. During the Franco-Prussian War, the area was the site of fierce fighting between French and German forces. Today, visitors can see several memorials and monuments dedicated to the soldiers who fought and died in the battles that took place in the area.

The Trocadero is also a popular spot for events and festivals. In the summer, the gardens host various concerts and shows, and during the winter months, there is an ice skating rink. The area is also home to several restaurants and cafes, offering visitors the chance to enjoy a meal or a drink while taking in the beautiful surroundings.

The Trocadero is also a great place to go for a walk or a jog. The gardens and surrounding areas are ideal for a leisurely stroll, and the views of the Eiffel Tower make for a memorable experience.

Chapter 15

Great Parks in Paris

Paris is known for its stunning architecture, rich history, and world-renowned cuisine, but it is also a city with an abundance of beautiful parks and gardens. These green spaces offer a peaceful retreat from the hustle and bustle of the city and provide a perfect spot for a picnic, a leisurely stroll, or simply a place to relax and enjoy nature. In this chapter, we will explore some of the most iconic parks and gardens of Paris.

1. Jardin des Tuileries: Located in the 1st arrondissement, this park was originally created in the 16th century for the Tuileries Palace. It features manicured gardens, fountains, sculptures, and a pond. Today, it is one of the most popular parks in Paris, with over 14 million visitors annually.

2. Jardin du Luxembourg: Located in the 6th arrondissement, this park was created in the early 17th century for the Luxembourg Palace. It features formal gardens,

an orchard, a pond, and numerous sculptures. It is also home to the French Senate.

3. Bois de Boulogne: Located in the 16th arrondissement, this park is one of the largest in Paris, covering over 2,000 acres. It features lakes, gardens, forests, sports facilities, and even an amusement park. It was originally a hunting ground for French royalty and was converted to a public park in the 19th century.

4. Bois de Vincennes: Located in the 12th arrondissement, this park is another large green space in Paris, covering over 2,400 acres. It features lakes, forests, gardens, and sports facilities. It was also originally a hunting ground for French royalty and was converted to a public park in the 19th century.

5. Parc des Buttes-Chaumont: Located in the 19th arrondissement, this park is known for its dramatic landscape, which features cliffs, a lake, and a suspension bridge. It also has a grotto, waterfalls, and a temple on a hilltop. It was created in the mid-19th century and is one of the most unique parks in Paris.

6. Parc Monceau: Located in the 8th arrondissement, this park is known for its English-style gardens, which feature curved paths, bridges, and a variety of plants and trees. It also has several sculptures and a pond. It was created in the 18th century and has been a public park since the 19th century.

7. Parc Montsouris: Located in the 14th arrondissement, this park features a lake, a waterfall, and numerous trees and plants. It also has several statues and a large lawn for picnics and sunbathing. It was created in the mid-19th century and is a popular spot for joggers and walkers.

8. Parc de la Villette: Located in the 19th arrondissement, this park is known for its modern architecture and design. It features numerous gardens, playgrounds, and sports facilities, as well as several theaters and cultural centers. It was created in the 1980s and is one of the most unique parks in Paris.

9. Parc de Belleville: Located in the 20th arrondissement, this park is known for its stunning views of Paris and its hilltop location. It features several gardens, waterfalls, and a large lawn for picnics and sunbathing. It was created in the 1980s and has become a popular spot for locals and tourists alike.

10. Square du Vert-Galant: Located on the Île de la Cité, this small park is known for its location at the tip of the island, overlooking the Seine River. It features several trees and benches and is a popular spot for romantic picnics and sunsets.

Chapter 16

Sunday: To Paris!

Our journey began with an unauthorized budget expenditure – choosing airport parking over the metro, which is in the budget, or a more expensive Uber. This $70 luggage-related decision, a lavish expense in our travel ledger, was a clever economic win, saving us from a $120 round trip in city transport to the airport. Yes, we could have gone for $2 per person on the metro closer to the terminal than the parking lot. Sometimes, when you travel, you have to make adjustments.

We imagined a seamless, elegant start as we embarked from the United States to Paris. Instead, a day peppered with comedic missteps and oddities unfolded, starting right at the airport. In our family, dietary restrictions are a preference and a way of life. This makes eating at airports akin to navigating a culinary minefield. Yet, on this day, fatigue and hunger led us to a unanimous, albeit rare, decision – airport food. The result? A chaotic symphony of half-eaten meals, none entirely satisfying anyone's palate. It was like musical chairs but with sandwiches. I got the bread from Mom's sandwich and the turkey from my daughters. My daughter used the cheese and lettuce to make a vegetarian sandwich. This culinary comedy was just a teaser for what awaited us at the gate and beyond.

Navigating Dulles International Airport is an experience that can only be likened to a level in a video game – think *The Legend of Zelda* but with more luggage. This complex labyrinth of tunnels, bridges, and trams was our real-life quest, filled with hurdles and unexpected plot twists. Among these was the TSA fiasco, a subplot that could easily have been lifted from a slapstick comedy. Despite the convenience of pre-checking, the process was anything but. My mother's TSA number had embarked on its own journey, vanishing from her ticket. This led to a frantic back-and-forth to the check-in desk, a scene that would have been hilarious if not for our ticking clock. Mom insisted she give her TSA number to the airlines and have it with her, but it was never printed on her ticket. It didn't matter to the TSA, who promptly sent her back through the super long line back to the check-in. Meanwhile, my daughter, the innocent architect of our liquid debacle, added her own flavor to the mix by trying to smuggle on shampoo *and* conditioner. When are we ever going to stop going through these absurd rules? And then there was me, selected for a special pat-down, a procedure that always seems to mistake my personal body composition (read: fat) for something far more sinister. I wanted to ask her if we should get drinks afterward, assuming we were dating then.

Once on the plane, our seating arrangement was a front-row ticket to an ongoing bathroom drama. Our non-reclining seats, adjacent to this high-traffic zone, became the epicenter of continuous disruption. The parade of passengers ranged from the desperately quiet to the unmistakably loud, with one unfortunate soul leaving behind an auditory memory we'd rather forget. And amidst this, the whispered rumors of an amorous adventure taking place within those cramped quarters added an element of absurdity to our already surreal experience. I didn't want to make eye contact, but I am not sure two people were in the cramped toilet. Can you join the Mile High Club as a solo act?

In a surprising plot twist, the in-flight meals turned out to be the unexpected heroes of our story. Our meticulously planned meal requests – vegan, vegetarian, and wheat-free – took an unscheduled detour, never making it to our tray tables. Instead, the alternative meals we were served were delightful culinary surprises. My lentil casserole, a simple dish, transformed into a gourmet experience at thirty thousand feet. This moment of unexpected gastronomic delight was a reminder that sometimes, the best experiences veer off the planned route. At least things were looking up.

As my family surrendered to sleep, their snores forming a harmonious backdrop to my wide-awake envy, I pondered the mysteries of comfortable airplane slumber. Watching them and the other passengers drift into peaceful oblivion, I couldn't help but feel a tinge of jealousy mixed with amusement at the irony of it all.

Our arrival in Paris was somewhat blurred (perhaps a side effect of my sleep-deprived state) but that's a tale for another chapter. With its unexpected laughter and lessons, this journey was the perfect prelude to our Parisian adventure. It served as a humorous reminder that travel is not just about the destination but also the delightfully imperfect journey that takes you there.

Chapter 17

Monday: Blurry-Eyed Sightseeing

I feel exhausted and unhappy after staying awake all night, trying to sleep. Instead, I watched too many Harry Potter movies on the flight to Paris. The tiredness caused by the long and sleepless journey has dampened the excitement of visiting the City of Light, at least for me. My family slept soundly beside me throughout the flight. By the time we landed, they were a little sleepy but raring to go. I usually consider myself a great traveler, but this time, I was beaten. All I wanted was a bed, but our check-in was not until 3 pm, and it wasn't even lunchtime yet.

Once off the plane, we found ourselves amidst long lines at the customs checkpoint for nearly an hour, eager to clear the formalities and start our adventure. The limits of my French studies became apparent as the waterfall of French falling from people's lips became a garbled stream of white noise. I could pick out a few words, but for the most part, I was word-blind in French. I hoped this was the product of sleep deprivation, but I was unsure. I thought my streak on Duolingo would be enough to get me some level of comfort. I was sadly very wrong.

Despite my tiredness and utter uselessness at French, we retrieved our bags swiftly, a small relief amid the chaos. Carrying baggage suitable for an expedition on the Silk Road, it became evident that taking the train to the hotel would be impractical. Our decision to opt for a car service proved beneficial, though it cost about €50. Nevertheless, the silver lining was that we had the opportunity to enjoy a delightful tour of the city on our way in, which helped lift our spirits and ignite a spark of excitement within us.

I must share a valuable tip if you're planning a trip to Paris. After collecting your baggage, look for the RAR train B to Paris. To facilitate convenient travel throughout the city, I highly recommend purchasing a Navigo Decouvert transit card at the transit window. This economical card costs only €30 per week and offers substantial savings, ensuring you can traverse the city's charming streets and iconic landmarks without worrying about transportation expenses.

Now, I must admit that my French language skills were far from impressive, and communicating with the locals posed a bit of a challenge. However, the people at the office were incredibly helpful, and despite the occasional confusion and gesturing, I managed to convey my needs. Bring a passport-style photo with those planning to get the Navigo card. Alternatively, you can pay eight euros for a photo to be taken and placed on the card. The €30 fee for the card covers your public transportation expenses for the entire week, including trips to and from the CDG airport, which typically costs around €12 each way.

As we ventured further into the bustling city, we quickly discovered that Parisian traffic and driving were in a league of their own. Having lived in various cities across the US, including New York, Los Angeles, and Washington, DC, I have experienced my fair share of chaotic traffic situations. However, the freeways and streets of Paris took the crown for being the craziest I had ever encountered. There were rules, but adherence to them seemed optional, at best. Lanes were merely suggestions, and turn signals were used sporadically. It was a unique and thrilling driving experience.

But let me be clear: if you plan on visiting Paris, renting a car is not recommended unless you are a seasoned driver with experience on the right side of the road. Public transportation in Paris is efficient and extensive, providing an excellent alternative to navigating the city's challenging traffic. Trust me; leaving the driving to the experts and using the well-connected Metro system to get around the city hassle-free is best.

Finally arriving at our hotel, we were warmly welcomed by the friendly staff, who offered to store our bags until check-in time. It was a welcome relief to remove the baggage, even temporarily. However, a bit of a mishap occurred when I realized that all the carefully prepared printed material with our itinerary, hotel address, and places to visit had been left inside the luggage. My exhaustion was apparent, having been awake for nearly 48 hours.

Grateful to finally arrive, my family was eager to satisfy our growling stomachs. We promptly searched for a nearby cafe on the illustrious Champs-Élysées. While the cafe offered stunning views and a charming ambiance, the culinary experience was underwhelming. Except for the scrambled eggs, a delightful surprise, the rest of the meal failed to meet our lofty expectations for our first taste of quintessential French cuisine. I am not sure what I expected, but this was not it. It would be the last meal I had on the grand boulevard. From here on out, it would be places filled with locals, not tourists. I can't prove this, but we were being punked. We then tipped at American levels, which is completely unnecessary, but we thought it completed the picture.

Afterwards, we stumbled out. .Not being a shopper myself, I observed my mother and daughter, both avid shoppers, revel in the luxury shopping opportunities along the Champs-Élysées. As they explored high-end designer stores, I focused on mentally mapping our surroundings to ensure we wouldn't lose our way in the bustling streets of Paris. It turned out to be a bit of an adventure, and my lack of fluency in French became evident as I tried to communicate with local salespeople who looked at me with pity and shame. They were willing to help, but I could not remember the French words for some makeup products and ended up gesturing in a strange makeup tutorial pantomime that did not bring us any closer to buying what we wanted. At one point in Sephora, they brought over someone who spoke German, thinking that my sad attempts at French were not French at all. Our trip was not off to a good start. Ultimately, my mother just handed them her Visa and said 'oui'. I am unsure if we got what we wanted, but it was still pretty good.

Our shopping expedition took us through high-end stores, jewelry boutiques, and tempting macaron shops. With every passing moment, I was reminded of the built-in 20% discount that visitors could enjoy through a VAT refund. It was a delightful surprise, akin to having every-thing on sale for us, making the shopping experience even more enticing. Try to put everything on your credit card and make sure. The rules are simple: personal retail purchases of €100.01 or more are eligible for a VAT refund. Purchases must be made on the same day in the same store. You can buy several items or just one thing if the receipt amounts to more than €100.01. Not every shop will offer VAT refunds, so ask first or ensure you get the *Detaxe* form to claim at the airport.

Despite the excitement, fatigue was taking its toll on me. I lost my sense of direction and mistakenly insisted that the hotel was on one street when it was actually on another. With no overseas phone service set up yet and my notes conveniently left in my luggage, navigating the streets became an amusing challenge. We ended up hailing a cab after wandering in circles for an hour. I forcefully insisted that I knew the hotel's location when I did not. I hadn't realized till then how important it was to set up the internet the second we arrived. I had all that time waiting in line at customs to set it up. Had I done that, it would have been a breeze.

Thankfully, it was soon time to check in at the hotel. It's common for hotel check-in to be around 3:00 pm, and with my family's symphony of snores echoing in the hotel lobby, we unintentionally secured an early access check-in and a room upgrade with a breathtaking Eiffel Tower view. The unexpected upgrade was a delightful surprise, and we felt pampered, almost as if the city welcomed us with open arms. The horrified hotel staff could not get us out of the lobby fast enough.

Stepping into our hotel room, we were greeted with a view of the iconic Eiffel Tower. The room exuded elegance and modernity, and the pristine bathroom with delightful shampoos, hand creams, and soaps made us feel like true Parisian guests. The bed seemed magical, inviting us into a world of sweet dreams and blissful slumber.

Despite the temptation to rest, my family's eagerness to continue exploring prevailed, especially as they had managed to get some sleep on the plane while I remained wide awake. My family headed out to get some takeout for us and to let me sleep. Not that I did sleep. I just stared at the walls and set up internet services on my phone.

After some time and an already blown itinerary, Mom laid down for a nap that she had not awakened for twelve hours. My daughter and I headed off on our own to the evening dinner and Eiffel Tower views at the Trocadero, with dinner at a nearby cafe afterward.

We were delighted to find that we could take just one bus to the Trocadero. We also could have taken the metro, but the buses run at regular and timely intervals and are included in our travel pass. The bus stop was right around the corner from the hotel, and the return bus stop was on the same street. You could not ask for better public transport, especially since it was included. It was great to travel above ground and get a short 10-minute driving tour of the city. It was insane driving around the Arc d'Triomphe, but the bus driver and all on board seemed unconcerned. I was terrified.

Over dinner, my daughter and I relished in conversations about our first day in Paris and shared our plans for the rest of the trip. We loved the great food and impeccable service. We found a cafe with a solid selection of French classics for very reasonable prices. We ate three courses each and had wine for under €50 per person. We laughed at our minor mishaps and reveled in the joy of being in such a captivating city. As the evening drew close, we returned to the hotel to find my mother still sleeping. In the morning, we would share our photos, and animatedly recounting our experiences made my mother feel like she had been part of every moment.

Day one in Paris came to a positive end with a wealth of unforgettable memories and a realization that despite the initial challenges, we were destined to have an extraordinary time exploring this enchanting city. As we settled into our comfortable beds, we eagerly looked forward to the following day, knowing that more wonders and discoveries awaited us in the captivating embrace of Paris.

Chapter 18

Tuesday: The Jewish Quarter

As the sun lazily began its ascent over the enchanting city of Paris, we decided to savor a well-deserved morning of relaxation. The previous day's adventures had left us feeling both exhilarated and a bit weary, so we opted to sleep in as much as possible. The comfortable beds at our hotel embraced us, luring us back into the realm of dreams for a few extra hours of rest.

When I finally crawled out of bed, I embarked on a mission to find the perfect breakfast treats, as we never opt for hotel breakfasts unless they are included in the room's price. I set out towards a nearby boulangerie renowned for its delectable croissants and pastries. The anticipation of sinking my teeth into these freshly baked delights made my stomach growl. I had many to choose from, and despite my irrevocably broken French, I managed to gesture to what I wanted.

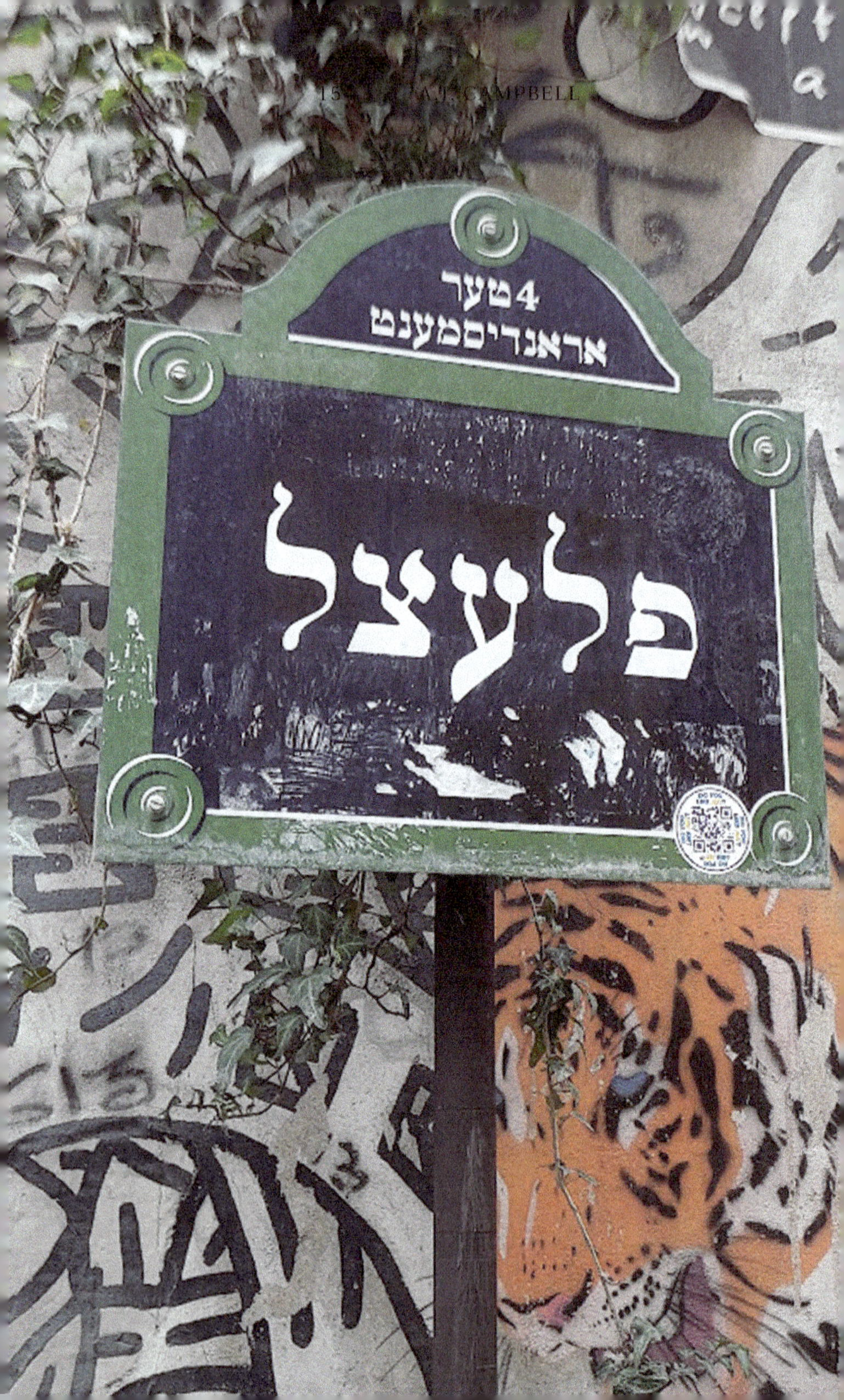

4 שער
אראנדיסמענט
פלעצל

On the way back, I wandered to the small supermarket next door to the hotel to pick up some butter and jam for the bread and pastries I was bringing back to the room. I tried to get out a few words in the supermarket, pointed a bit, grabbed some fruit and a yogurt or two, and returned to the room. I thought my French was better than this. I feel like I didn't do my homework despite working an hour a day for 100 days plus the two years in high school.

We had some hotel room coffee, which was surprisingly good. Then we took turns getting ready, from my speedy 10-minute routine to a full face of makeup with consultation on shoes, hats, and coats.

It was almost 10:00 am when we headed out the metro to the day's first stop, where we would buy our four-day museum pass. Museums in Paris have heavy admissions fees, so taking advantage of a museum pass is a great cost-saving tip. We used the four-day pass for €70 (parismuse-umpass.fr/t-en). The days are back-to-back and are of great value, as well as museums; there are admissions to other attractions like the Eiffel Tower and the Arc de Triomphe.

You only get one admission per venue for the duration of the pass, so if you want to spend days at the Louvre, it might not be the best fit for you, but if you are looking to survey many museums, then this pass will likely save you money. Admission to the Louvre is €17 alone, the Palace of Versailles is €24 for a pass, and the Arc de Triomphe is €13. Using a pass can save you time, but it still means you have work to do. Many places will require a time slot reservation in advance. Check the museum website for details.

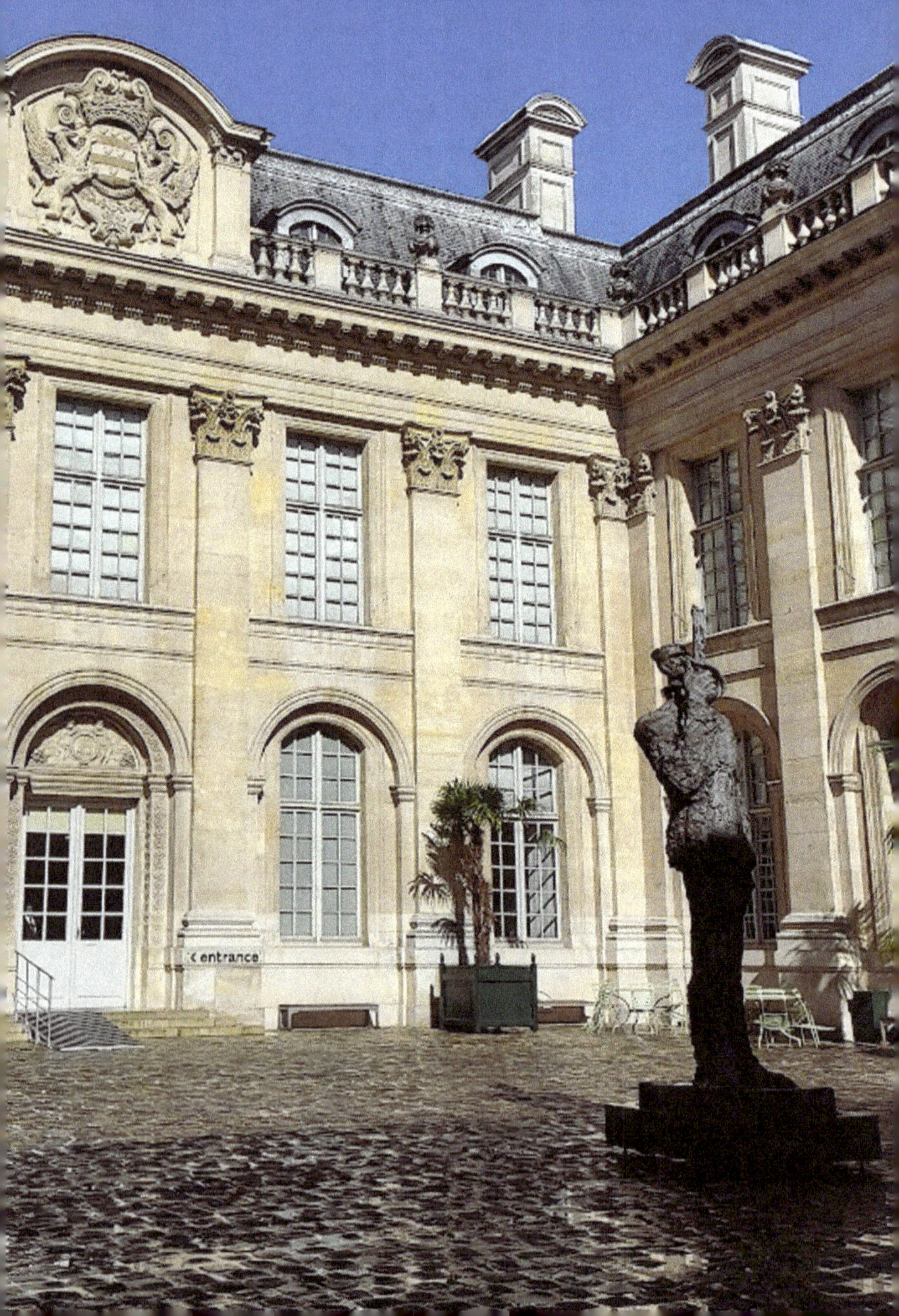
entrance

The Jewish Quarter

Jewish history in Paris is a rich tapestry that spans centuries, reflecting both the cultural vibrancy and the challenges faced by the Jewish community in the French capital. From the early medieval period to the present day, Jews have played a significant role in the development of Parisian cultural, economic, and intellectual life while also facing periods of persecution and discrimination.

The earliest records of Jews in Paris date back to the 6th century. The community grew over time, contributing significantly to the city's economic development, particularly in trade and finance. The Middle Ages were a tumultuous period marked by expulsions and readmissions. The most notable expulsion occurred in 1394 when Charles VI ordered all Jews to leave France, a decree that lasted until the French Revolution.

The French Revolution in 1789 was a turning point, as it led to the emancipation of the Jews. They were granted French citizenship and legal equality, which allowed the community to flourish. The 19th century saw a significant increase in the Jewish population of Paris due to immigration, especially from Eastern Europe and the Mediterranean region. This period was characterized by a thriving cultural life, with contributions to literature, art, and science.

However, the 20th century brought new challenges. The Dreyfus Affair in the late 19th and early 20th century exposed the deep-seated antisemitism in French society. This was followed by the horrors of World War II and the Holocaust, during which thousands of Parisian Jews were deported and murdered by the Nazis and their collaborators.

In the post-war period, the Jewish community in Paris began to rebuild. Today, Paris hosts a vibrant and diverse Jewish population with a rich cultural life, including synagogues, schools, and cultural institutions. The community contributes significantly to Paris's social, cultural, and political fabric while remembering and honoring its complex and often painful history.

The Musée d'Art et d'Histoire du Judaïsme or mahJ (mahj.org/en) offers a glimpse into the city's rich Jewish heritage and history, providing a meaningful and educational experience for all of us. The exhibits at the museum were enlightening, and we found ourselves engrossed in the stories and artifacts that showcased the profound impact of the Jewish community on the cultural tapestry of Paris.

The museum is located in the heart of the Marais District, "the Swamp," right on rue du Temple, in the 3rd Arrondissement of Paris, and a short walk from the Pompidou Centre. The nearest metro stations are Rambuteau (line 11) or Hôtel de Ville (lines 1 and 11). Jews originally settled in the Marias during the Middle Ages. There are thousands of years of Jewish presence in Paris across many neighborhoods.

If you are looking for more sites and memorials, consider the following:

1. Mémorial de la Shoah: 17 rue Geoffroy l'Asnier, *memorialdelashoah.org*
2. Chir Hadach: 1 rue des Hospitalières-St-Gervais, *librairiedutemple.fr*
3. Diasporama: 20 rue des Rosiers, *diasporama.com*
4. La Foire du Livre: 37 rue Richer, *lafoiredulivre.com*
5. Kosher Restaurants: *kosherinfrance.com*

6. Offices of the Association Consistoriale Israélite de Paris: 17 and 19 rue St-Georges, *consistoire.org*
7. The Synagogue Buffault (Orthodox): 28 rue Buffault, *buffault.net*
8. The Synagogue de la Victoire (The Grand Synagogue): 44 rue de la Victoire, *lavictoire.org/English/*

After delving into the history at the museum, our stomachs began to remind us that it was time for lunch. We embarked on a culinary adventure in the charming neighborhood of Pletzl, the traditional Jewish Quarter. With its eclectic blend of cultures and flavors, this area promised a treat for our taste buds. Pletzl is a Yiddish term meaning "district" or "neighborhood". You'll want to get off at Metro Saint-Paul (Line 1) and walk three blocks to the area. Or you could wander around like we did.

We decided to try some Chez Marianne (2 rue des Hospitalières Saint-Gervais, 75004 Paris), a popular spot known for its delightful cuisine. The dishes were an explosion of flavors, leaving us wanting more. We felt like real Jewish Parisians drinking wine and eating delightful recipes of Shasuka and Falafel.

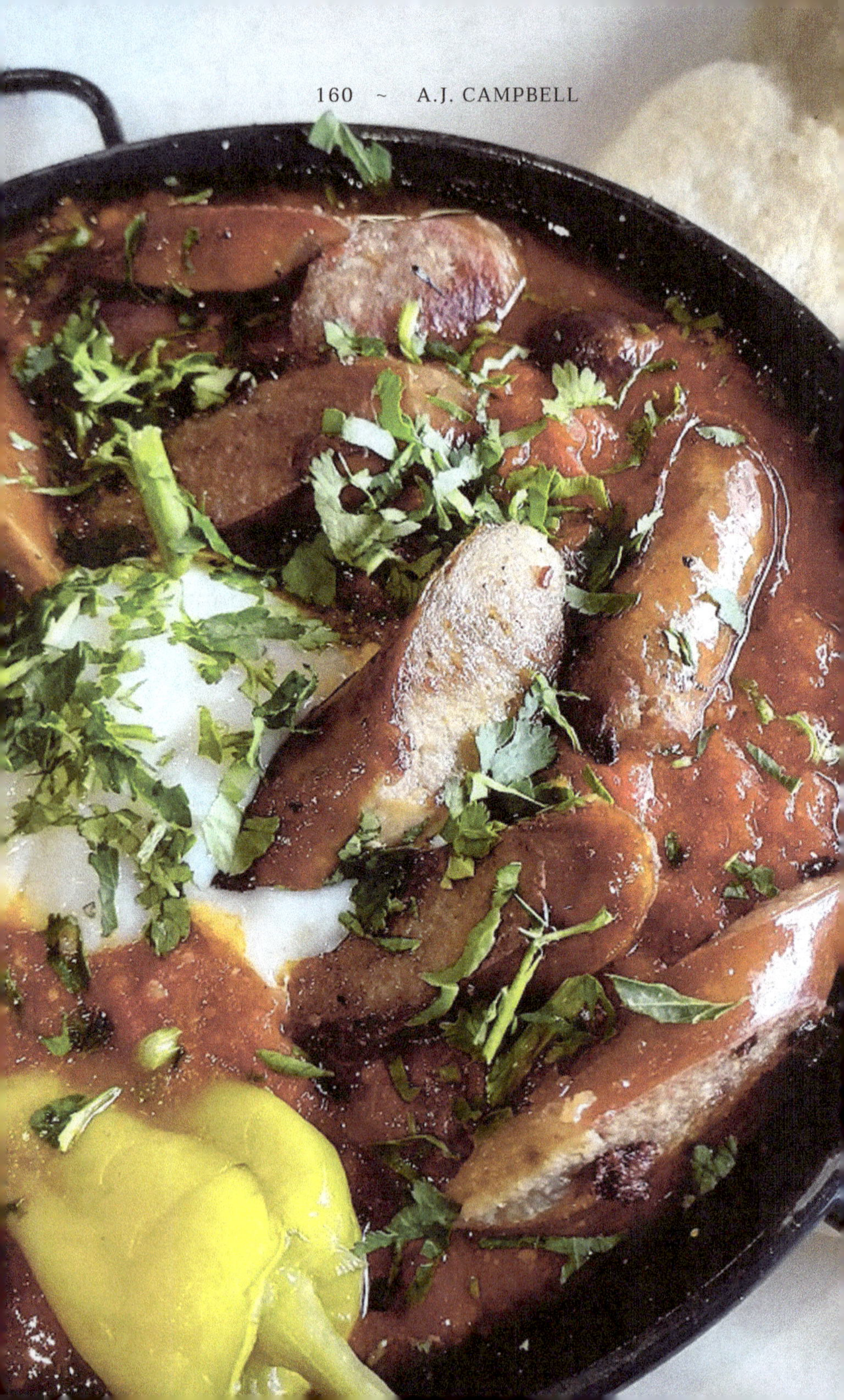

It's also important to take in the moving plaques outside the area's schools, which pay somber tribute to Jewish children and former students deported to death camps during World War II. One of the most prominent of these can be found on the rue des Hospitalières-Saint-Gervais, a pedestrian street just off rue des Rosiers.

Of course, no meal is complete without something sweet to end on a high note. An adorable bakery caught our eye near the restaurant and bookshop, Korcarz (Kosher) (29 rue des Rosiers, 75004 Paris, korcarz.business.site), offering an assortment of cookies and cakes. We couldn't resist grabbing some treats for a quick dessert, a few cookies, and some to return to the hotel room.

Right outside the bakery was one of the memorials to the forced deportation of French Jews. Sadly, you can find such plaques outside buildings in many Parisian neighborhoods—especially in the 10th, 11th, 18th, 19th, and 20th arrondissements, where many French Jewish citizens lived before 1940. The one pictured in the photo with the red door describes the family that occupied the house before the Nazis removed them with complicity from the French Vichy government.

Here Lived Baruch and Dora Matykanski Their daughter Ester (9 years old), deported in 1942 by the Nazis with the active complicity of the Vichy government and exterminated at the Aushcwitz camp because they were Jewish.
In their memory.

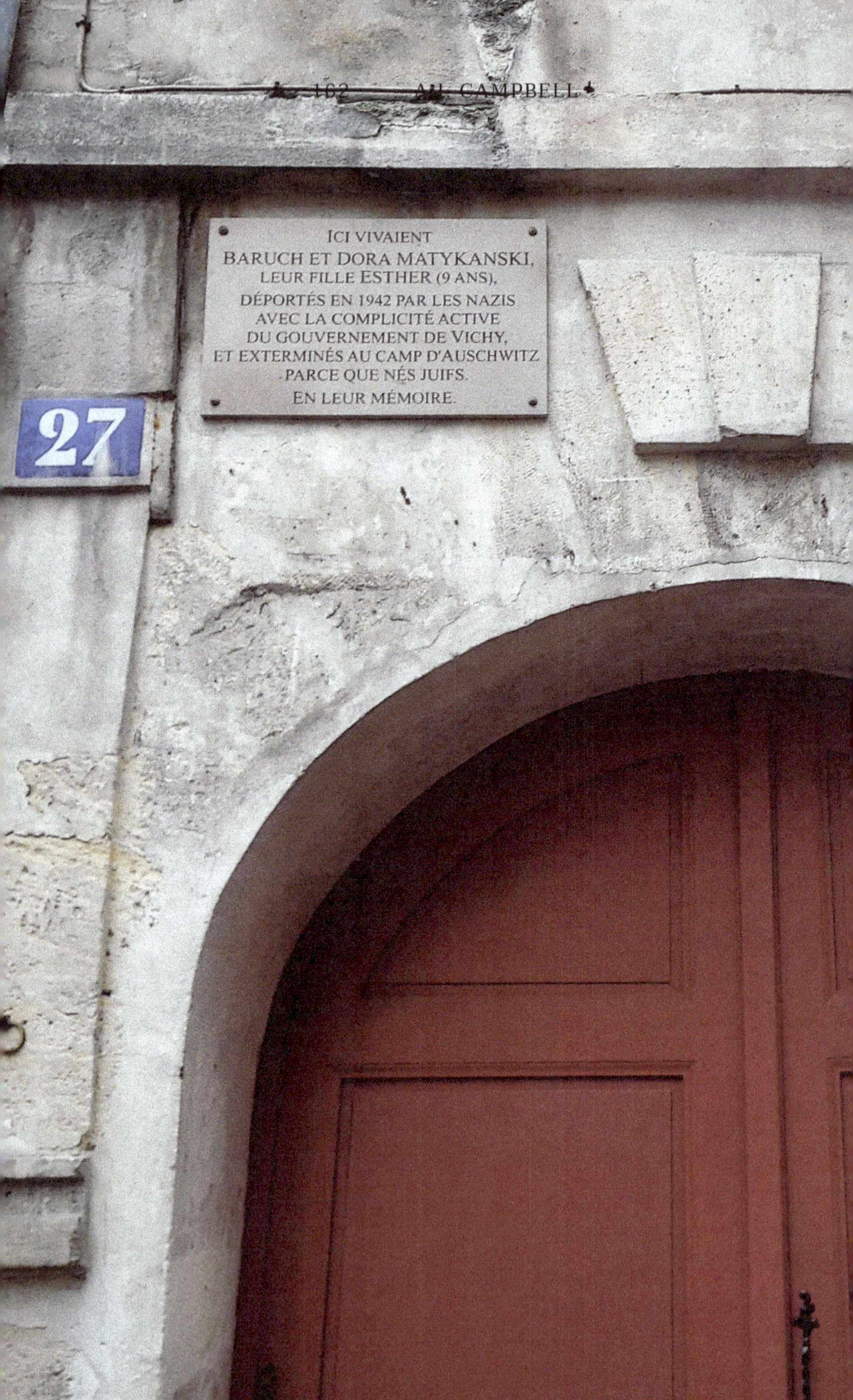
27
ICI VIVAIENT
BARUCH ET DORA MATYKANSKI,
LEUR FILLE ESTHER (9 ANS),
DÉPORTÉS EN 1942 PAR LES NAZIS
AVEC LA COMPLICITÉ ACTIVE
DU GOUVERNEMENT DE VICHY,
ET EXTERMINÉS AU CAMP D'AUSCHWITZ
PARCE QUE NÉS JUIFS.
EN LEUR MÉMOIRE.

Exploring the Shops

We were transformed in the Marais through its history and into the fashionable district it has become. It embodies a perfect blend of old-world charm and contemporary flair. It is renowned for its vibrant LGBTQ+ community, trendy boutiques, and art galleries, making it a cultural hotspot in Paris. The district's narrow, winding streets are lined with pre-revolutionary buildings and classical architecture, offering a visual feast for history enthusiasts and photographers alike.

We shopped for discount and vintage clothes at the thrift shops and spent time in the fashionable clothing stories. We found some amazing bargains for high-quality second-hand fashions. Shopping in these stores gave us a sense of how the locals shop. Most people we spoke to said they chose some high-end items for their wardrobe, like coats and blazers, but they would mix it with a lower-end thrifted Levi's or a high street t-shirt with a second-hand scarf and purse. Eclectic is in, and getting the most fashion for your dollar is the key to French fashion success.

With our cravings satiated, we strolled through the streets, exploring the funky shops that lined the district. Each store offered a unique and artistic touch, making every corner a treasure trove of surprises.

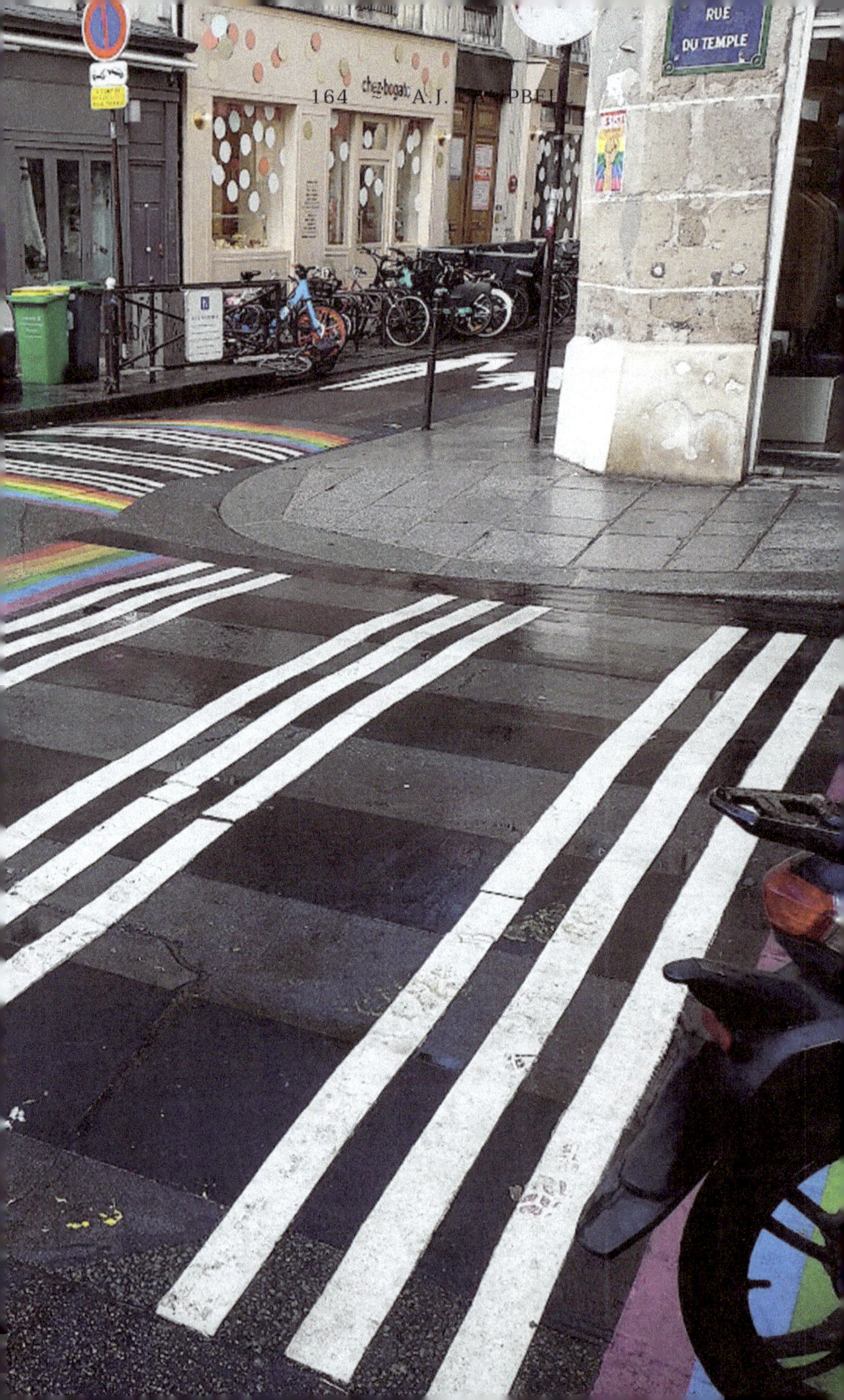
RUE
DU TEMPLE
164 chez bogato A.J. CAMPBELL

Afternoon

As the afternoon sun bathed the city in golden hues, we decided to head back to our hotel for a brief respite. Resting in the comfort of our rooms, we recharged our energy for the rest of the day's adventures.

With the clock ticking towards 5:30 pm, we prepared to embark on a breathtaking experience. Our destination was the magnificent Arc de Triomphe, an iconic symbol of French history and resilience. The panoramic views from the top of the monument promised a stunning visual feast, capturing the essence of Paris from every angle.

It is beautiful to photograph the outside, but the real joy is taking pictures from the roof after wheezing our way up the spiral staircase that nearly put me into a hospital bed. There are elevators for those who need it (details are available at paris-arc-de-triomphe.fr/en/visit/practical-information and or paris-arc-de-triomphe.fr/visiter/visiteurs-en-situation-de-handicap). If you have any conditions that would benefit from the elevator, stand firm and ask for it. It was not a joke. The small spiral staircase and the speed one takes were challenging for every family member. When I discovered an available elevator, I asked about it and was told I should take the stairs anyway because it is healthy for me. If you need the elevator, insist on taking the elevator.

I was completely out of breath as we reached the top, but I was determined to get a great picture, including the Eiffel Tower. The sun began its descent on the horizon, painting the sky in hues of orange and pink. The sight of the Eiffel Tower in the distance, standing tall and proud, took our breath away. We watched as the city transformed from day to night, with the twinkling lights below resembling a sea of stars.

Camera shutters clicked continuously as we aimed to capture the beauty of this moment forever. We stayed until after sunset, relishing every second of the spectacular vista that unfolded before our eyes. It was the kind of evening that one dreams of when you think about Paris. Yet, as I looked around, I saw other tourists missing the view while trying to get the perfect picture for their Instagram. Women with multiple outfits tried to look glamorous in a flowy sundress on a cold evening. All these people missed the reason for being there: to enjoy the scenery and breathe. It is a time for me to enjoy my family and marvel at the ingenuity of humanity, where we work together to make amazing things happen, building over time brick by brick, improving, and learning as we go.

When we descended, we were met with a beautiful chorus of young soldiers singing at the Tomb of the Unknown Soldier and Eternal Flame. It was a moving tribute to the fallen sung by young soldiers who probably had not been deployed yet. Their voices were lifted and rebounded under the Arc, filling the area with a beautiful harmony.

We wandered around after the choir disbursed, taking photos outside the Arc before heading for dinner. Paris was in the middle of a transit slowdown, so the buses were full, and we had to wait a long time only to find an overcrowded bus. My mom bounded on to the bus and urged my daughter and I to do the same, but there was no room. My daughter and I headed to the previously agreed upon restaurant on foot, which got us there before the bus arrived. Sometimes, it is just faster to walk.

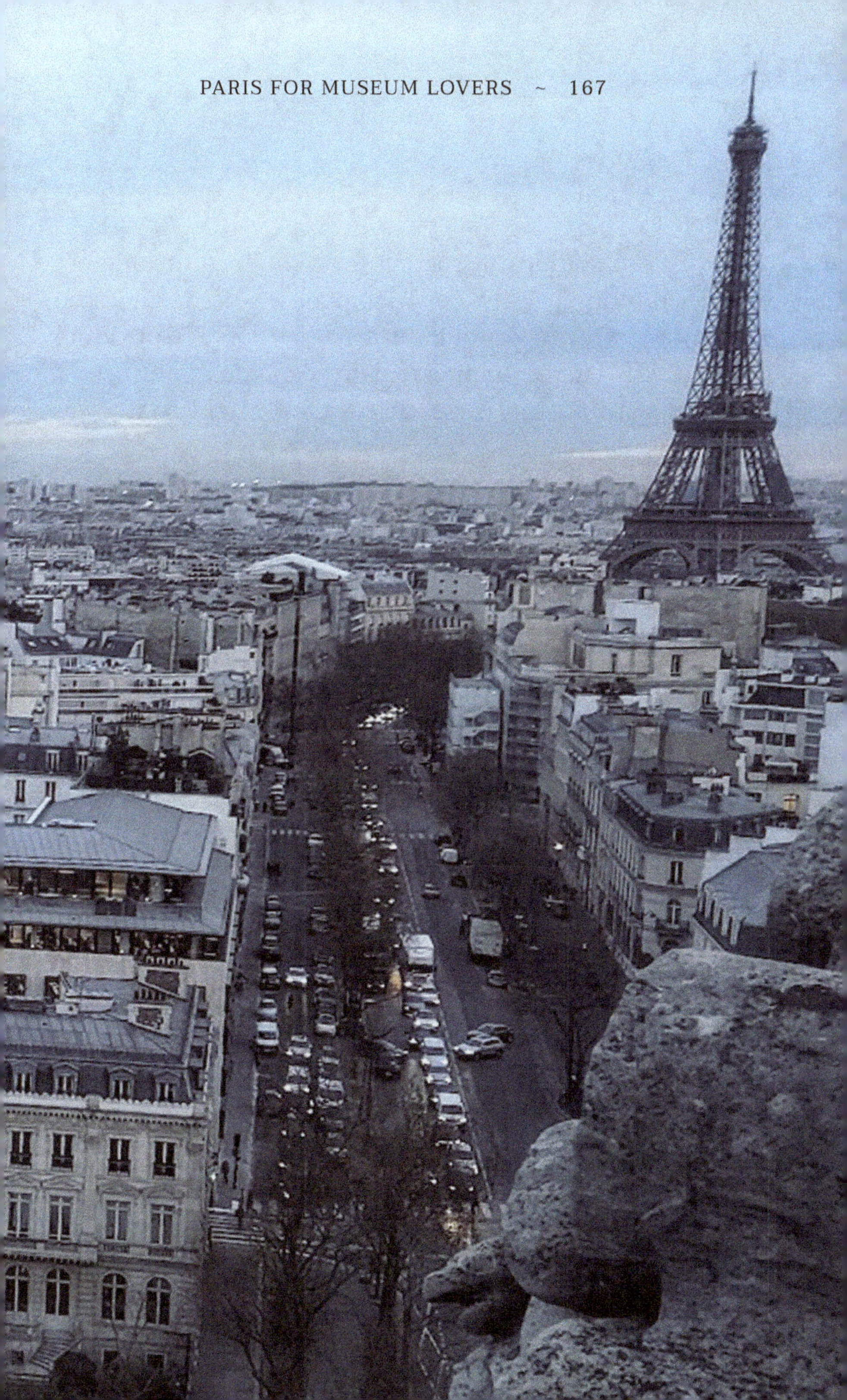

Dinner

With our spirits still soaring from the breathtaking experience atop the Arc de Triomphe, we headed for the restaurant where we would wait for my mom. Our desire for a classic Parisian dining experience led us to Elysee St Honore, conveniently located just a few blocks away from the iconic monument and our hotel.

The ambiance of the brasserie exuded a timeless charm, and the menu boasted an array of delectable French dishes. The tantalizing aroma of the dishes filled the air, setting the stage for a memorable dining experience. Be prepared to pay €26 per plate for the main with starters in the €10 to 15 range, which we split. We spend quite a bit at dinner but skimp during the day when we are sightseeing. We linger over long dinners and have sandwiches for lunch at the museums or on the go. While we did have lunch in the Pletzel today, it would not be our experience for the rest of the trip. Call it a special splash out.

As we savored every bite, we relished the camaraderie and laughter accompanying the meal. The warm glow of the restaurant's lights added to the cozy atmosphere, making us feel right at home in the heart of Paris.

Our day came to a close with hearts and stomachs full, leaving us eager to discover even more of the city's wonders in the days to come. With each new adventure, Paris continued to weave its magic around us, leaving an indelible mark on our souls. As we retreated to our hotel for a night of blissful sleep, we knew that this journey through the City of Light was only beginning.

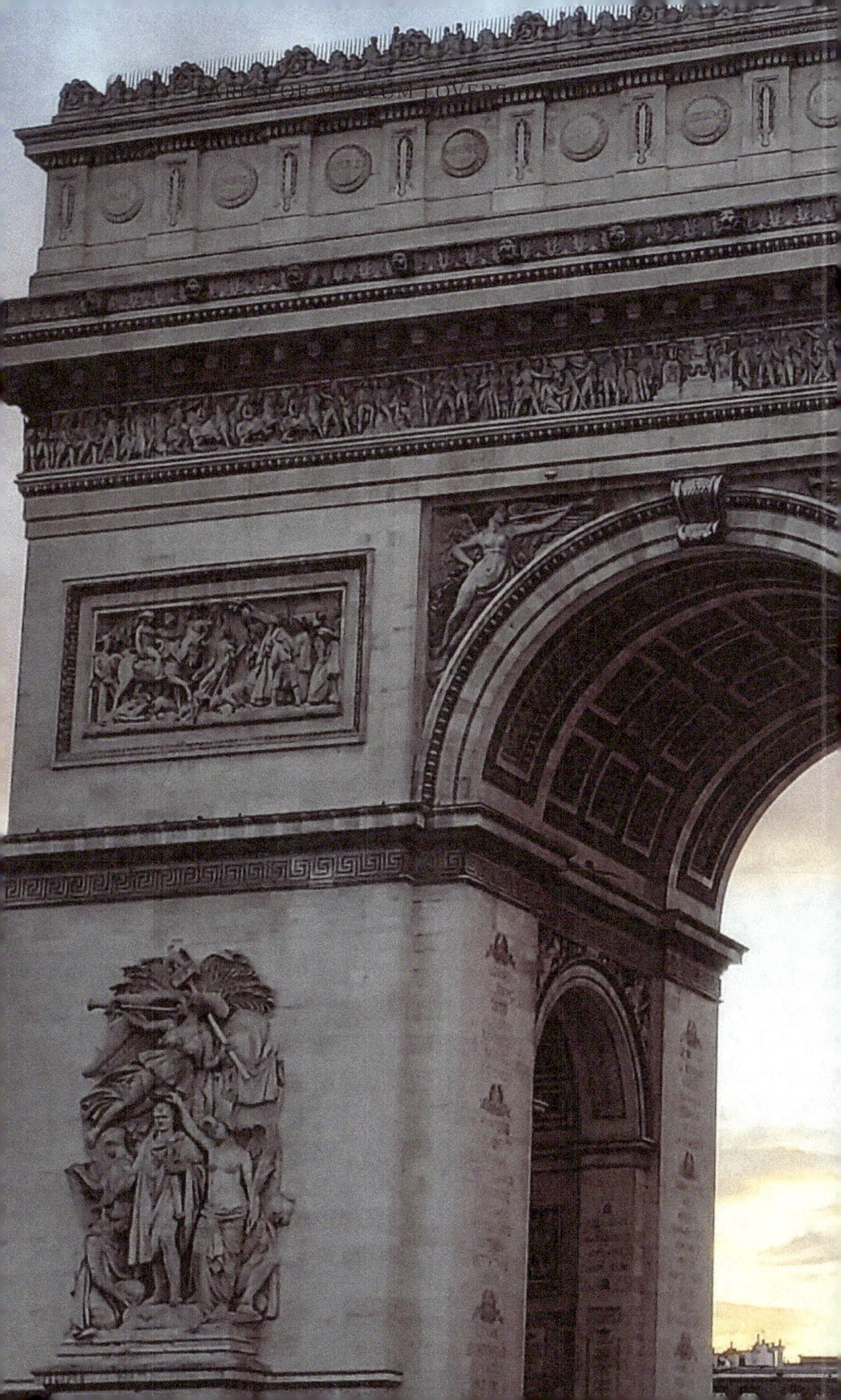

Chapter 19

Wednesday: The Louvre

As the first rays of the morning sun lazily stretch over Paris, I peel myself out of my cozy hotel bed to the delightful cacophony of my mom and daughter, who absolutely, positively do not snore. On the other hand, I have been known to shake the walls with my nocturnal symphonies.

My snoring was so bad on this trip that I was forced to seek refuge on the floor in the hallway. Yes, I slept on the floor before the door, with the bedroom door firmly closed. It was a perfect setup: I could barely hear my family snoring over my own racket, so everyone was happy.

When I wake up early, as I almost always do, it's completely silent, over the snoring. This is my cue to venture out and procure fresh pastries, ready to embrace a day filled with art, history, and the inevitable tourist clichés. The hotel's attempt at charm with a spread of pastries and coffee sets the tone for the day's escapade. Nothing screams "authentic Paris experience" like croissants on a platter served with smooshed pastries and runny eggs.

I tell myself to just keep walking. Nothing in my life has been so bad that neither I nor my non-snoring family deserve the hotel breakfast. Instead, I walk through the smelly streets of Paris's 8th arrondissement amidst the stench of garbage left uncollected for almost a week following the strikes. I will say there are surprisingly few rats, given that the trash buffet is wide open. It is a mystery, but not such a great mystery as how men keep their jackets balanced on their shoulders all day without falling off. Some things we will never find out.

My French is getting a little better, but I have noticed that I get strange looks when I try to speak. I can only assume that my language-learning app has failed a bit. I am like *Emily in Paris,* who, after years, still can't speak French. But I trek on to the bakery, dodging the curiously hygienic-looking trash.

I chose the croissants from Le Pain du Faubourg (165 rue du Faubourg Saint-Honoré, 75008 Paris, France). It is a little pocket of a bakery shop that doesn't open on weekends. You will find quiche, tarts, meringues, and fresh sandwiches ready to go by 9 am. Shops like this are all over and are an inexpensive way to take a bite out of Parisian life.

Morning at the Louvre

Before we headed out, my family got ready, and I strategized our Louvre invasion like a general plotting a major battle. We had our Paris Passes ready because who wants to waste precious sightseeing time standing in queues when there's art to be superficially admired? Armed with sandwiches from a local boulangerie – because lugging around bread all day is what makes you truly Parisian – and various fruits and chips from the nearest supermarket, we set off on our grand adventure.

Of course, in true tourist fashion, I made a rookie mistake that I'm sure many have made before me. Despite having a reservation to enter and our Paris Passes for tickets, I didn't follow the wise advice of travel bloggers to go through the Carrousel du Louvre. This underground shopping mall is very posh and has almost no walk-in line to the Louvre. But no, I had to be the maverick, find a line, and stand in it. It was cold, a little damp, and altogether miserable, but after 45 minutes of shivering and questioning my life choices, we finally got through security.

Once inside the Louvre, we heeded the sage advice to use the coat check. Storing our belongings, including our gourmet lunch, we freed ourselves from the cumbersome bags. After all, nothing should distract us from our mission to nod knowingly at art pieces and take the perfect selfie.

The Louvre's magnificence comes with an obligatory warning about the crowds. The sight of so many people crammed together in the name of culture can be over-whelming. To avoid a cultural stampede, we focused on a curated list of must-see pieces: the captivating *Winged Victory of Samothrace*, the iconic *Venus de Milo*, and the enigmatic *Mona Lisa*. Because it's basically illegal to visit the Louvre and not elbow your way through a mob to see her smirk.

We got the audio guide, which should be reserved in advance, and then promptly only used it once while waiting in line for the Mona Lisa. "La Joconde," which translates to "the joyful one" or "the happy one" in English, is derived from the Italian term "La Gioconda," referring to Lisa Gherardini, the wife of Francesco del Giocondo. We were decidedly less happy waiting in line to see the masterpiece, but it gave us time to view the paintings in the room and listen to some of the audio we would eventually put aside. The closeness of the crowds made the headphones feel stifling, like a sensory overload in the vastness of the museum.

We were more on a mission to see the breadth of the museum rather than dig down to learn, which I think is perfectly okay. I wish we had spent a week at the Louvre, but we didn't have more than five hours. Mom wanted to see some of the decorative arts, so we dodged the bulk of the crowds to check out the Napoleon III Apartments (Appartements Napoléon III). These opulent rooms are part of the museum's decorative arts collection and showcase the lavish lifestyle of the Second French Empire under Napoleon III. The sheer grandeur was enough to make us momentarily forget the hordes of people and feel like we had stepped into an episode of *MTV Cribs*.

Afternoon Exploration

As midday approaches, the allure of our packed lunch becomes irresistible. We find a spot inside the iconic Louvre Pyramid, surrounded by art and a sea of fellow picnickers. We dig into our sandwiches, savoring each bite and congratulating ourselves on this culinary triumph. A sip of water here, a bite of bread there, and we're ready to dive back into the art world.

Replenished and re-energized, we continue our adventure through the Louvre's halls and galleries. Each section reveals new treasures from different eras and cultures, leaving us in awe of human creativity and history's knack for accumulating dust.

No Louvre visit is complete without exploring the historical battle hallways. Paintings depicting significant historical moments are powerfully emotional, capturing the essence of human drama and the complexities of our past. Or at least, that's what the brochure says.

Throughout the afternoon, I silently thank myself for exploring the Louvre at my own pace, allowing me to soak in the art's intricacies without the pressure of a tour guide's schedule. Wandering through the grand halls, I find the Louvre's atmosphere both humbling and inspiring as a museum lover.

Evening Delights

After a day of art-filled enrichment, it's time to head back to the hotel; our minds and camera galleries full of Louvre memories. The museum has left an indelible mark on my heart, but we needed a break from all the walking. I know that Americans are obsessed with steps but I think Parisians could double or triple our daily steps.

As evening approaches, we are drawn to a charming spot: Café de l'Avenue at 190 Bd Haussmann, 75008 Paris. The cozy ambiance, warm lighting, and welcoming atmosphere create the perfect setting for unwinding. We settle in with refreshing drinks and a charcuterie board featuring an assortment of cured meats, cheeses, and delectable accompaniments. Each bite celebrates French culinary prowess, even if it is just fancy finger food.

Sharing stories and impressions of the day, we bask in a sense of deep fulfillment. From the sumptuous breakfast to the mesmerizing art and the delightful dinner, the day has been a whirlwind of Parisian experiences, all tied together with a bow of snark and sarcasm.

As the night sky envelops Paris, the city comes alive with its unique energy. We might explore the vibrant night-life, soaking in the beauty of illuminated landmarks and charming streets. Or we might just return to the hotel for a well-deserved rest, knowing that today's memories will be treasured – or at least talked about – for a lifetime.

A day in Paris centered around the Louvre is a magical experience. From the moment you indulge in delightful pastries and coffee to the awe-inspiring journey through the world's largest art museum, the day celebrates human creativity, history, and culture.

Exploring the Louvre at your own pace, engaging in clever banter with your companions, and savoring local treats allows for a deeply personal connection with this iconic city. As you bid farewell to Paris, you carry a treasure trove of memories, a newfound appreciation for art, and a longing to return to the City of Light someday. And perhaps a slight annoyance at the crowds, but that's all part of the charm.

The allure of Paris, with its rich history, captivating art, and exquisite cuisine, ensures that every visit is unique and unforgettable. Whether it's your first time or a return trip, Paris continues to beckon travelers with its timeless charm and everlasting allure – and just the right amount of witty commentary.

Chapter 20

Thursday: A Royal Escapade to Versailles

The sun gently filters through the curtains, glowing warmly in our cozy and increasingly cluttered room. We were forever looking for phone chargers, gloves, and hairbrushes. Organization in the room is important to keep everyone moving along and reduce stress. I would strongly recommend a ten-minute round of room cleaning before departing in the morning for your day's fun.

The trip is about one hour from where we stayed in the 8th. We took the 9 train to Alma-Marceau to the RER C train to Versailles Château Rive Gauche. We exited from the metro station and crossed the bridge to the train station. You can also take the 171 bus Château de Versailles from Pont de Sèvres, which will drop you right at the front gates.

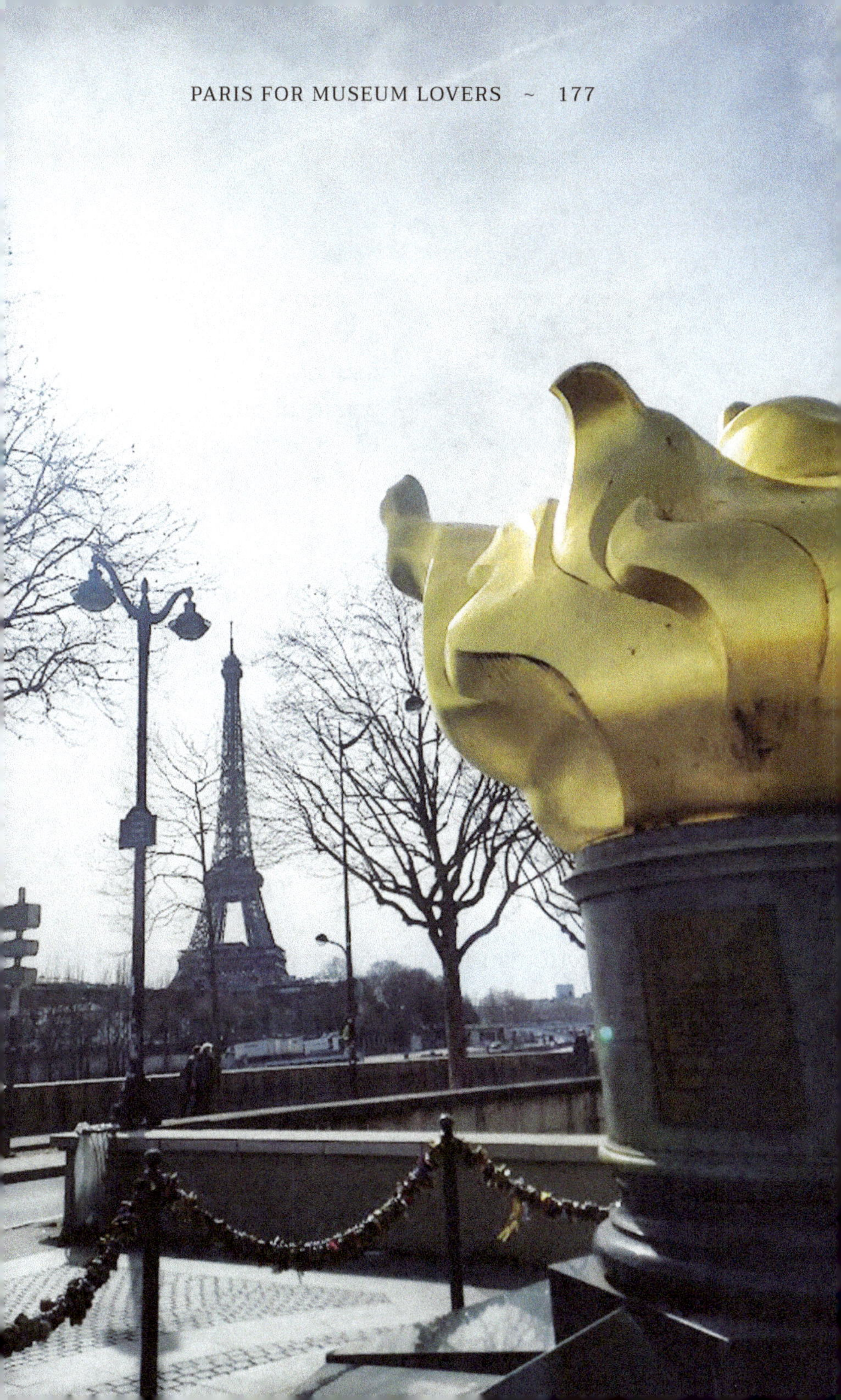

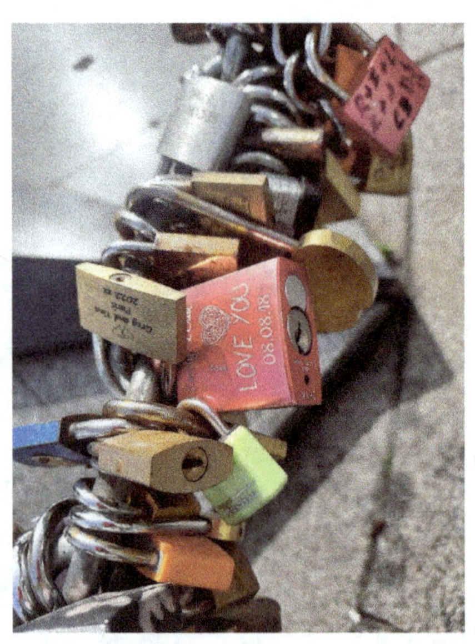

Before you cross the bridge, you should stop for a moment and appreciate the beautiful and loving tribute to Princess Diana above the underground tunnel where she died. Out of love for the Princess, lovers and those missing someone dear have had locks engraved and locked on the chain sur-rounding the memorial. Stop for a moment and read a few of the locks. You will see that love is an eternal flame and lives in her memory.

Walk a little further and cross the Pont de l'Alma, a road bridge in Paris, France, across the Seine. It was named to commemorate the Battle of Alma during the Crimean War, in which the Ottoman-Franco-British alliance achieved victory over the Russian army in 1854. It is a beautiful arched bridge that is wonderful to take photographs of the Seine.

A quick few-minute walk across the bridge brings you to the train station, where you will find the RER C. You should not have to wait that long for a train as they are frequent. We used the CityMapper app quite a bit and Google Maps to supplement. It was a short wait before the lovely double-decker commuter train headed out to the suburbs and the Palace of Versailles. Tickets are usually between 3-5 Euros.

There are other trains to Versailles, so please check the palace website or the travel apps for the best option.

It was a beautiful 30-minute train trip using our Navigo Pass through wonderful towns, each with a slightly different feel. As the urban slipped away to the suburban, I got a feel about how life around Paris is very similar to my own life living around Washington, DC, in a small leafy suburban town driven by working in the city and living in the suburbs. Travel, in every way, brings out the big tableau and the small worlds that live inside of them.

As the train approaches the royal city of Versailles, you will think you are in any other train station. But don't worry, it will get much better. After you exit the station, you will have a ten-minute walk to Versailles. Don't worry about taking a cab unless you need mobility assistance.

You can already feel its historic charm enveloping you the second you turn the corner and see the grand visits to the palace. It is like nothing you have ever seen, but simultaneously, totally underwhelming. The bulk of the palace is hidden, and you will not appreciate the enormity of it all until you are inside and roaming.

Thanks to your Paris Museum Pass, the admission is already handled, but reservations are mandatory. After a quick security check, you find yourself amidst a crowd of visitors, all eager to immerse themselves in the opulence of this iconic landmark. But we arrived early, so we zipped through the security line briefly and were let free in the building and grounds that my mother agreed to understated elegance. Many of her furnishings are reproductions of items we saw inside the palace. I am sure Marie Antoinette would approve of my mother's sitting room.

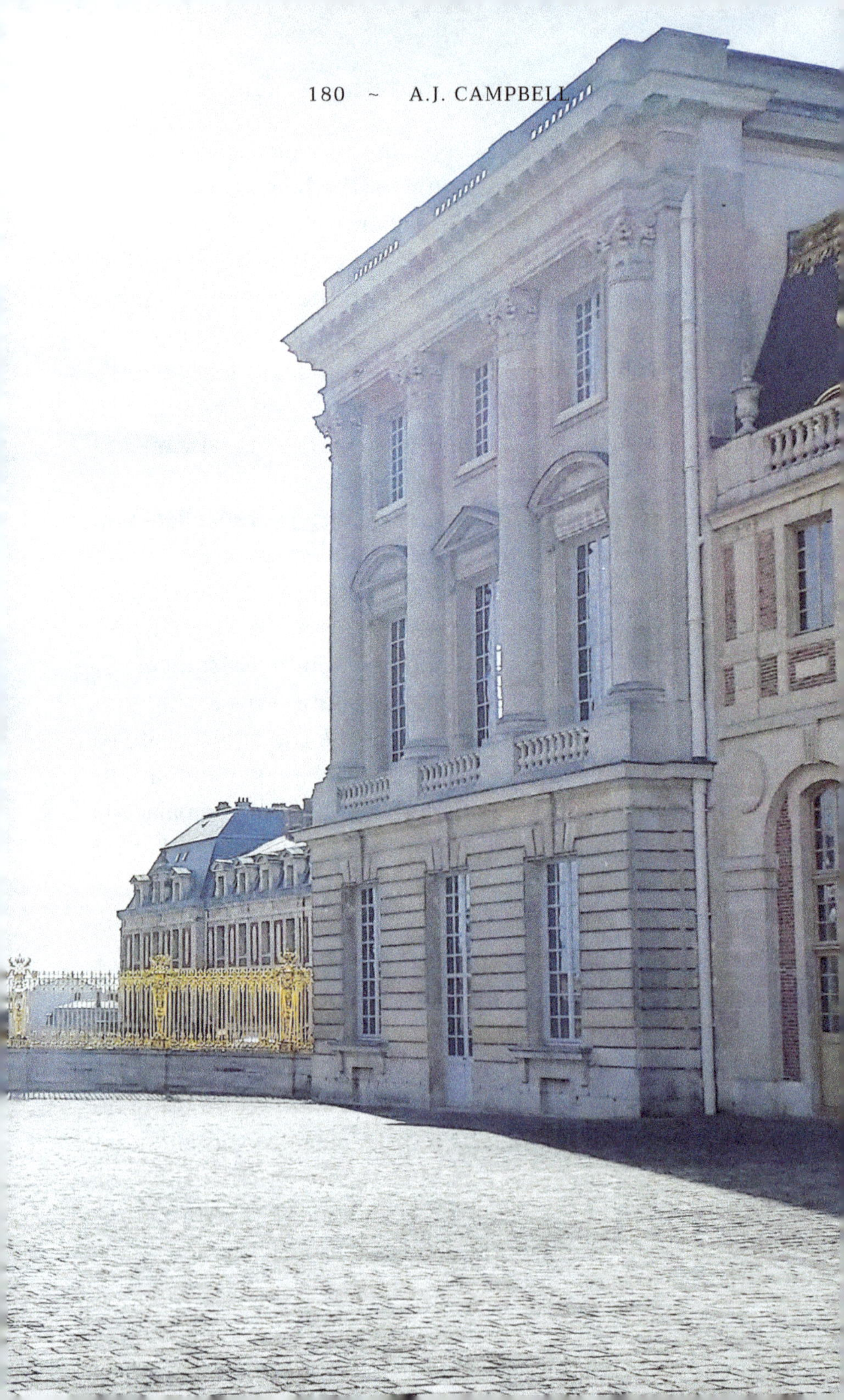

We wandered endlessly through the Palace and missed the Hall of Mirrors and the hot chocolate at Angeline's restaurant. There is too much to take in all at once. It is overwhelming to the point that it becomes a blur. I had to focus on just one thing or risk ignoring it all, so I focused just on the door knobs. I know that is silly, but the locks were incredibly ornate and represented privacy from the rest of the court. The door knobs don't have to be as fancy as they were, but detail was added to make them pretty. It speaks to the craftsmen who made them and the desire to turn the ordinary into the extraordinary. If you want to know more about the locks, a person cobbled a blogspot about them. I am not sure why this is not a coffee table book available at the gift shop, but it should be (thisisversaillesmadame.blogspot.com). We stopped for a break before heading out to the gardens.

All the opulence in the Palace, while people starved in the streets, was truly shocking. I assume this is my typical American reaction to monarchy, but this Palace was supposed to be a hunting lodge before becoming the main palace and seat of government in 1682. I felt like a French revolutionary running into the Palace for the first time and seeing how much of their money was diverted from their pockets to this opulence. My American sensibilities aside, we have palaces in America, too, and they were built much more recently.

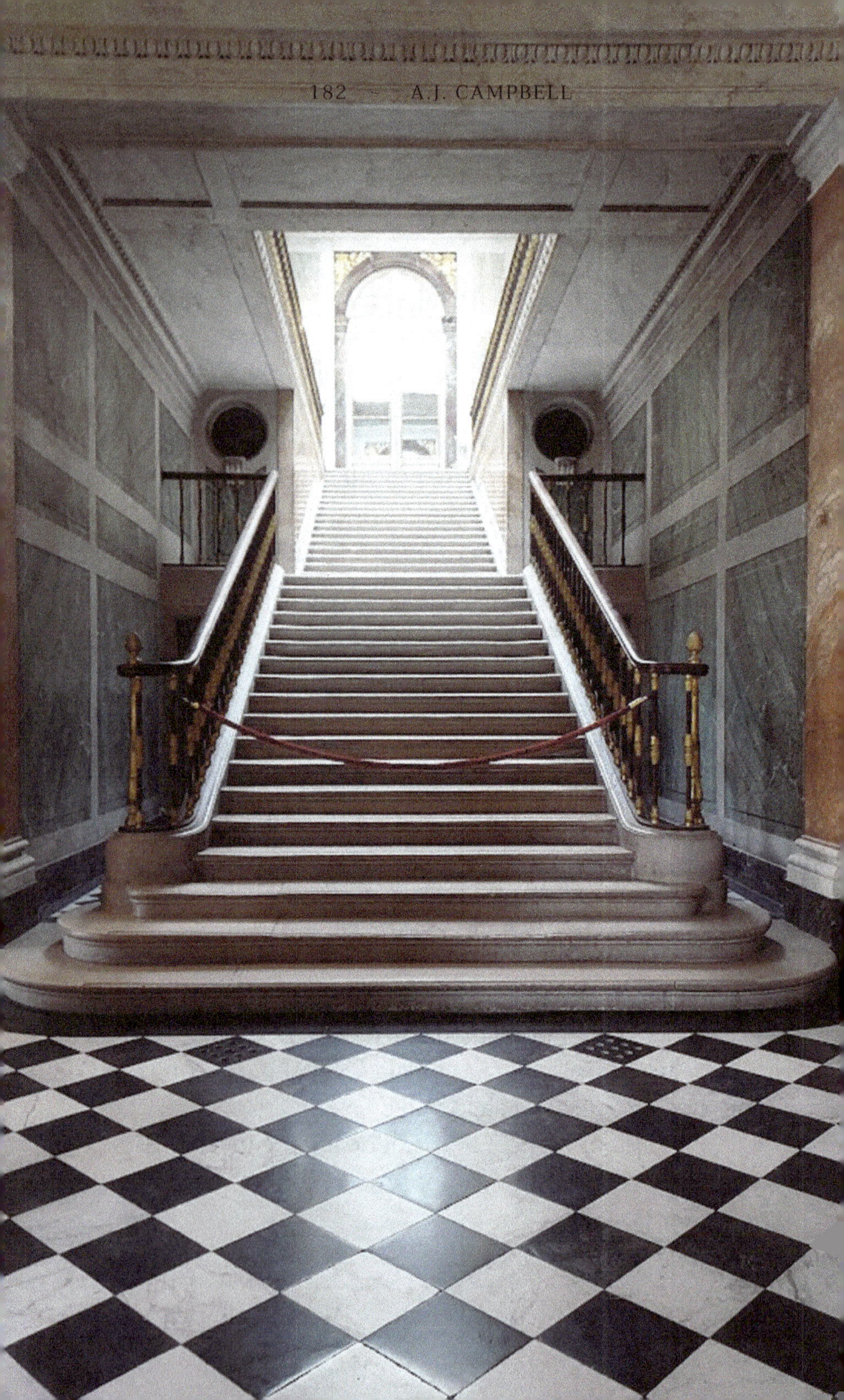

We were overwhelmed by the money it took to build this place. Touring our Whitehouse does not resemble anything like this. But, of course, American wealth is not displayed in the government but in the houses of the wealthiest of its citizens. A quick tour of the Biltmore estate in North Carolina would rival at least parts of Versailles, on which much of its style is based.

Although, if I am honest, after the Louvre the day before and the tour of the Apartments Napoléon III and now Versaille, I think I had just had my fill of the decorative arts. I vowed next time to focus more on the historical artwork and history of the paintings and sculptures to make a more balanced perspective. If you are lucky enough to show up on a weekend, you can tour the carriage house full of, you know, guided carriages. We didn't see it, but I would aim to do that next time.

Into the Gardens

I sincerely underestimated the need to reserve a golf cart to tour the gardens in advance. My family has mobility challenges, and walking all day and then attempting to tour the gardens was way too much for all of us. However, we went there early and were able to take a golf cart for 40 euros. It was so well worth the price.

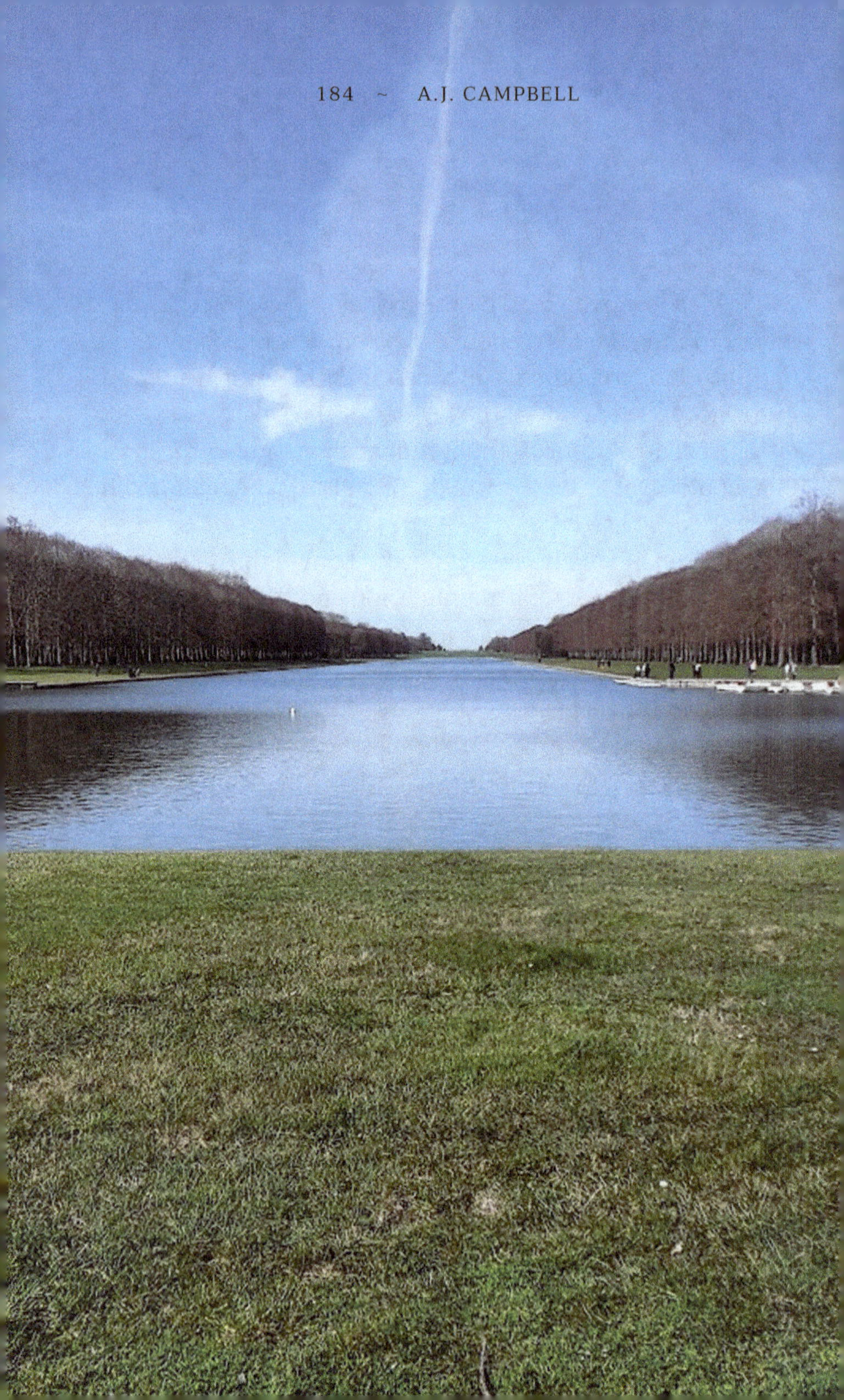

We drove all over the grounds with the wind in our hair and a map in our hand. We relish the freedom to roam and discover hidden corners of the stunning gardens and lakes. One hour is hardly enough, even with the golf cart. We did manage to stop for a bit by the Petit Trianon for lunch. We had bought sandwiches at the boulangerie on the way out for 6 or 7 euros and just took them with us, hoping we would have a place to eat. We were not disappointed.

When you eventually find the perfect spot, perhaps a picturesque spot by the serene lake or amidst the blooming grand gardens, you settle down for a delightful picnic. We felt like French royalty out on a picnic in a little carriage.

Afternoon

Having indulged in the majesty of Versailles, it's time to return to the lively streets of Paris. You can hop on the train once again, or if you prefer a more accessible bus, you have that option, too. While leaving the enchanting palace behind, you can't help but feel grateful for the opportunity to witness the splendor of French history up close. You will find the 171 bus right outside the gates on the first bus stop you see headed back to the train station.

Looking back, I realize how much I walked on these high-intensity days. When you return to the hotel room, change your socks and shoes before heading out again. Your feet will thank you for it.

Dinner

As the evening sets in and our excitement for the day slowly transforms into contentment, the thought of a delectable dinner crosses our minds. We ran into the local brasserie, Brasserie L'Alsace (restaurantalsace.com/en/), as if it were our grandmother's house and she was calling dinner. Check out the menu before heading out, as the fish-heavy menu might not be everyone's favorite. You will find it right next to the big Five Guys burger joint.

I can't imagine going to Paris just for a burger I can get at home, but I know some people like to compare fast food in different countries. For example, in Paris, McDonald's offered vegetable fries made of carrots, beets, and parsnips instead of potatoes. They looked like a bouquet of colored fries, but people seemed to like them. Check the McDonald's France website; they are not to be seen (mcdonalds.fr/).

As Thursday draws to a close, you can't help but reflect on the wonders you've experienced throughout the day. From the elegant charm of Versailles to the delightful dinner at Brasserie L'Alsace, this day has been a perfect blend of history, culture, and gastronomy. Each moment has left an indelible mark on your journey through France, making you eager for Friday's adventures in the City of Lights.

Chapter 21

Friday: Musee d'Orsay

We had coffee and pastries in the hotel room, but if you are feeling like splashing out, you can head to La Pâtisserie du Meurice par Cédric Grolet near the entrance to Jardin des Tuileries at 6 rue de Castiglione, 75001 Paris. It is an elevated pâtisserie with trompe l'oeil marzipan, and delightful deserts served like jewelry under glass. The pâtisserie is part of the Dorchester Collection (dorchestercollection.com/paris/le-meurice/dining/la-patisserie-du-meurice-par-cedric-grolet).

We knew today would be busy and did not have time to stop, as we had so much on our plates. It was off early through the Jardin des Tuileries, over the Seine, to the Musee d'Orsay, and then to the Paris Catacombs.

We exited the Concorde train station and walked to the Jardin des Tuileries on the way to the Musée d'Orsay. If you have time to have lunch or coffee in this beautiful garden, please make the

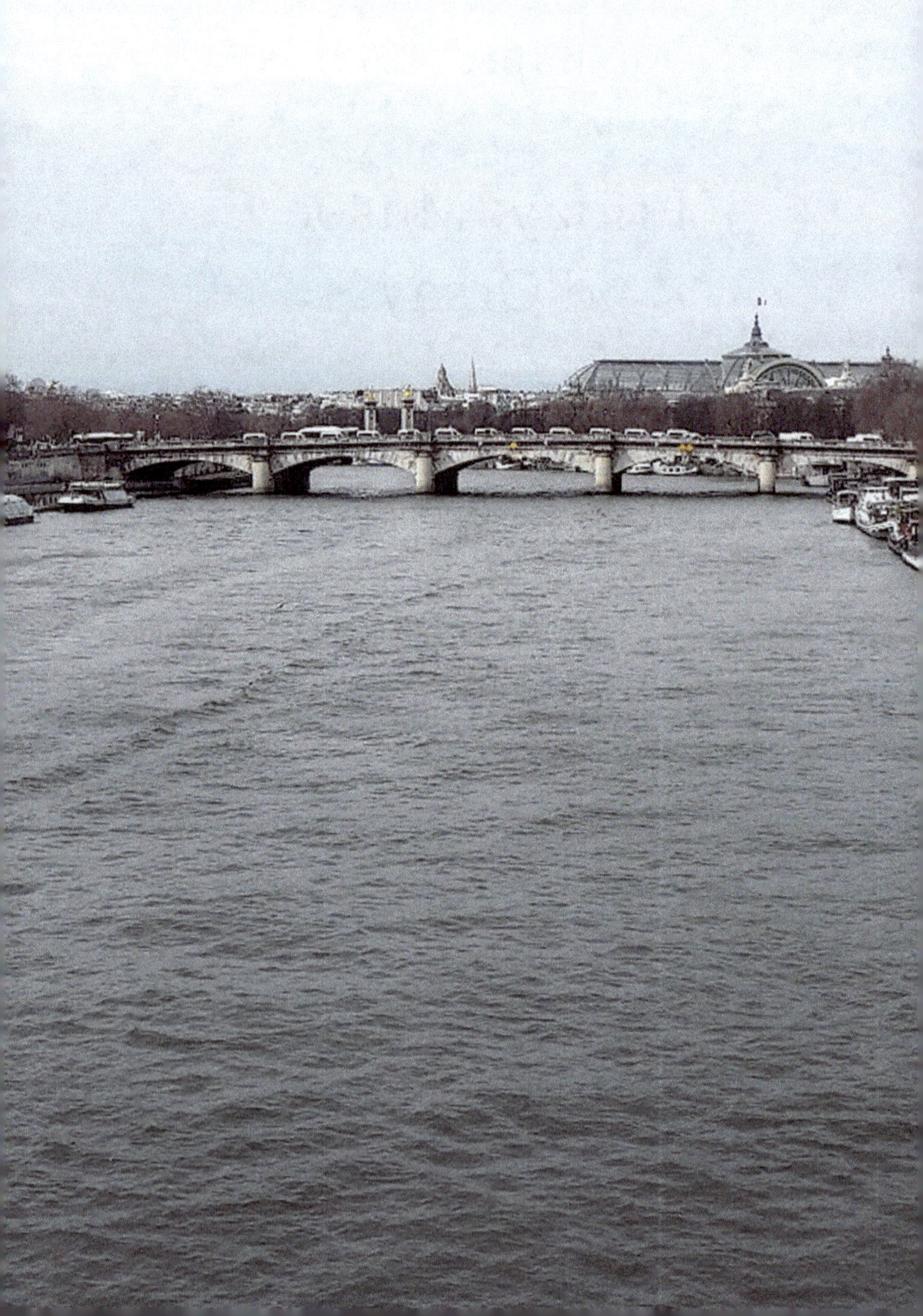

time. It is not to be missed. There is a smaller museum near the Concorde train station inside the garden called Jeu de Paume, an Arts center for photography & video from the 19th to 21st centuries, with avant-garde exhibits.

Another Tulleires museum you might find delightful is the Musée de l'Orangerie in the top of the garden closer to the Seine. The museum has a 20th-century European art collection, showcasing 8 of Monet's water lilies murals. Check out the current offerings at musee-orangerie.fr/en.

Tuileries Garden

The Tuileries Garden, located between the Louvre and the Place de la Concorde in the 1st arrondissement of Paris, France, is a public garden with a rich history dating back to the 16th century. Created by Catherine de' Medici in 1564 as the garden of the Tuileries Palace, it was opened to the public in 1667 and became a public park after the French Revolution. Since the 19th century, it has been a place for Parisians to celebrate, meet, stroll, and relax.

The Italian Garden of Catherine de' Medici (16th Century)

Catherine de' Medici commissioned the original garden in the Italian Renaissance style. It was an enclosed space with various plants, fountains, and sculptures, designed to be a peaceful retreat from the city.

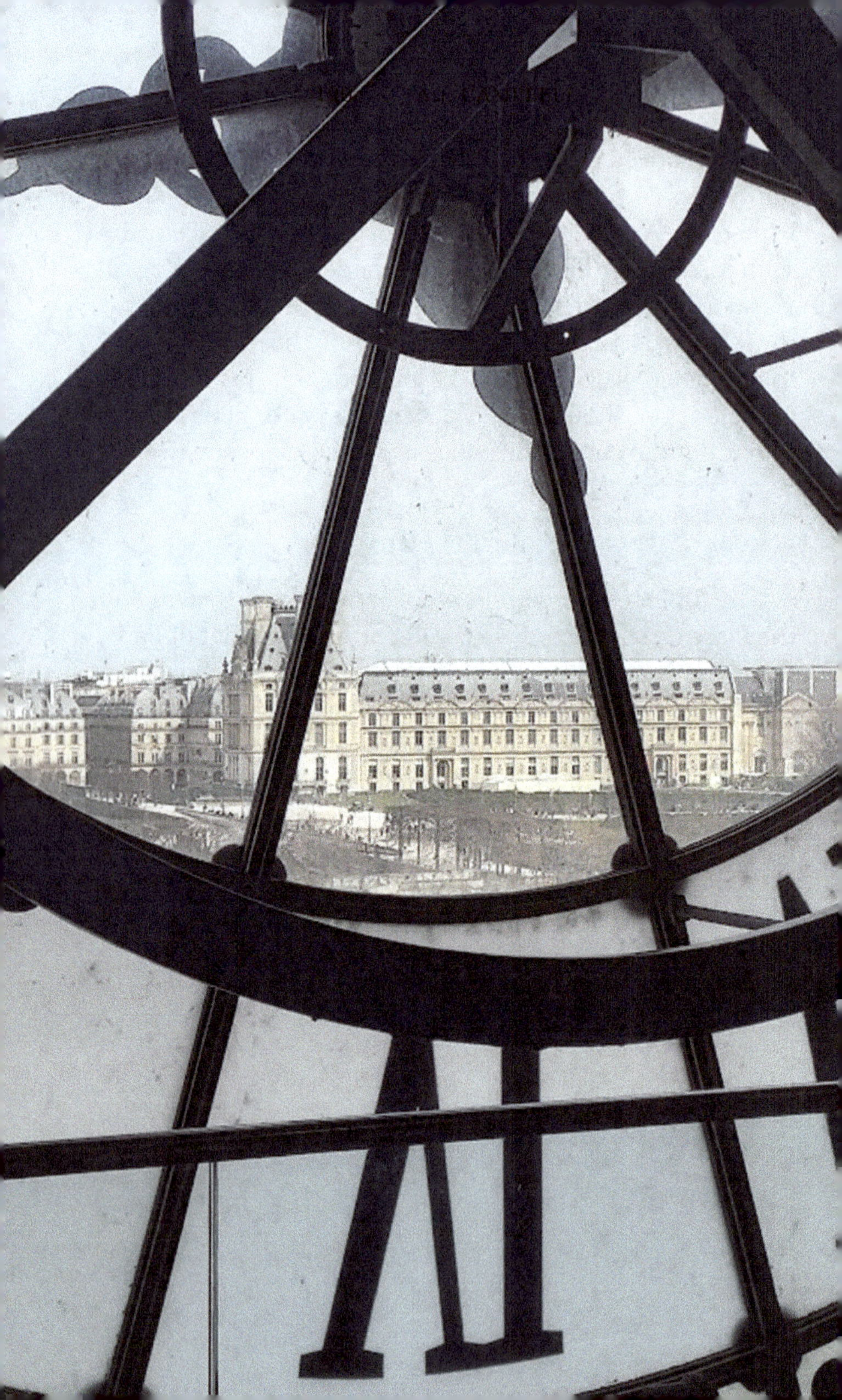

Garden of Louis XIII and Louis XIV – The French Formal Garden (17th Century)

The garden transformed Louis XIV, who introduced the French formal garden style. This style was characterized by its symmetry, order, and long perspectives. André Le Nôtre, the famous landscape architect, was responsible for redesigning the Tuileries Garden in this style.

Louis XV and Louis XVI – Changes and Events

The garden continued to evolve during the reigns of Louis XV and Louis XVI. It became a venue for events, including balloon flights and revolutionary ceremonies. The garden's layout and design were further modified, reflecting the changing tastes and politics of the time.

Early 19th Century – The Garden of Napoleon and the Restoration

In the early 19th century, during the reign of Napoleon and the subsequent Restoration period, the Tuileries Garden underwent further changes. During this time, the garden started to take on its modern form.

Concerts and Promenades - The Garden of Louis-Napoleon and the Third Republic

Under Louis-Napoleon and during the Third Republic, the Tuileries Garden became a place for concerts and promenades. It was increasingly seen as a public space for

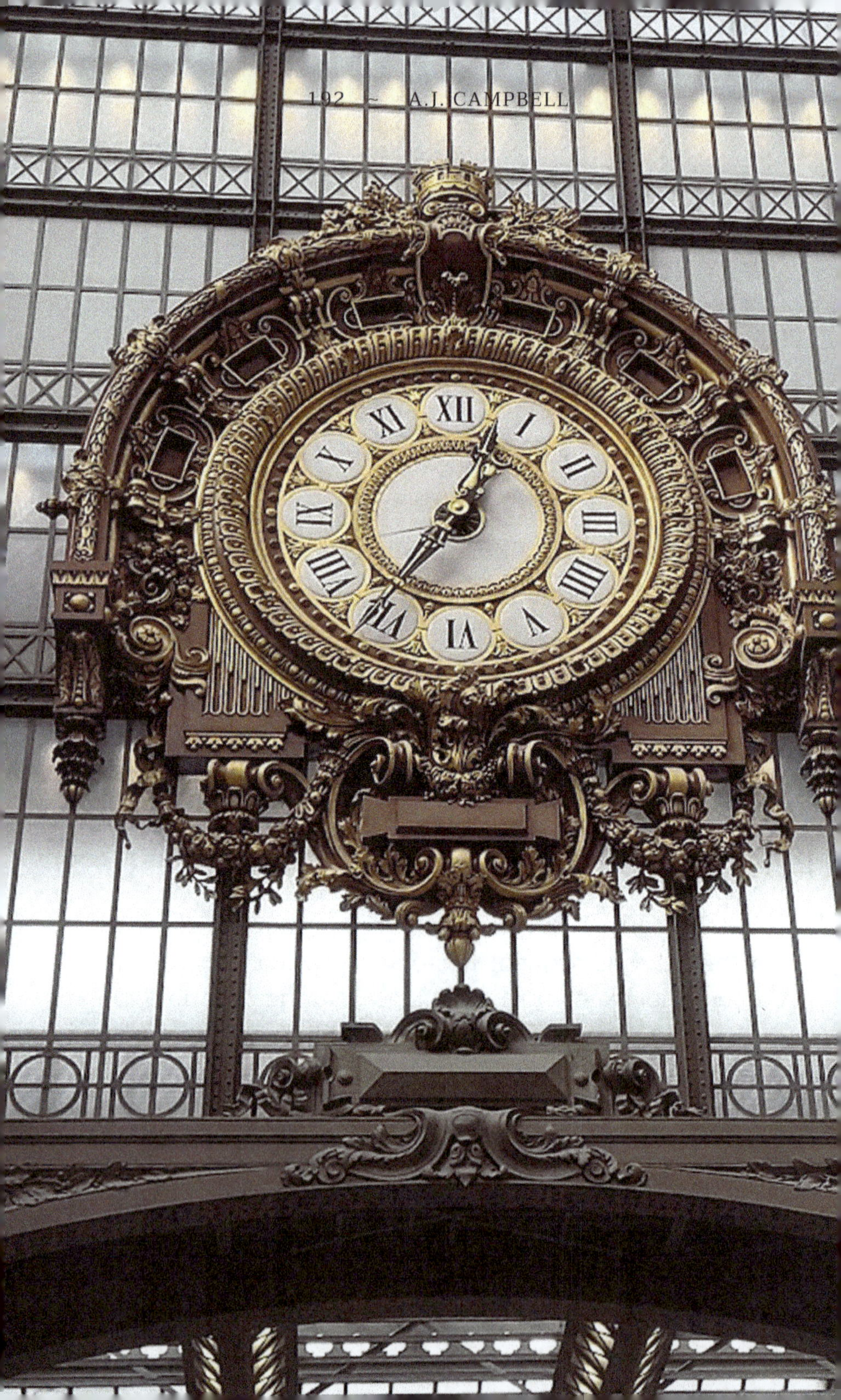

leisure and entertainment, reflecting the democratization of society.

20th and 21st Century – Restoration and Updating

In the 20th and 21st centuries, the Tuileries Garden has been restored and updated. Efforts have been made to preserve its historical layout while introducing modern amenities and restoring historical features.

The Tuileries Garden, with its long history, has witnessed many significant historical events in France. From its origins as a royal garden to its current status as a beloved public park, it reflects the cultural, political, and aesthetic changes that have shaped Paris over the centuries. The garden is a green oasis in the city's heart and a living monument to French garden design and urban planning history.

Musée d'Orsay

The Musée d'Orsay, located on the Left Bank of the Seine, is a museum housed in the former Gare d'Orsay, a Beaux-Arts railway station built between 1898 and 1900. The museum primarily features French art dating from 1848 to 1914, including paintings, sculptures, furniture, and photography. It is renowned for holding the world's largest collection of Impressionist and post-Impressionist masterpieces, with works by artists such as Morisot, Monet, Manet, Degas, Renoir, Cézanne, Seurat, Sisley, Gauguin, and van Gogh. Many of these works were previously housed at the Galerie Nationale du Jeu de Paume before the museum's opening in 1986. The Musée d'Orsay is one of the largest art museums in Europe.

The building that now houses the Musée d'Orsay was originally a railway station, Gare d'Orsay. It was built on the site of the Palais d'Orsay and was designed by architects Lucien Magne, Émile Bénard, and Victor Laloux for the Chemin de Fer de Paris à Orléans. The station was completed in time for the 1900 Exposition Universelle. Despite being a modern innovation at the time, the design of Gare d'Orsay was considered an anachronism, as it drew inspiration from the past, masking the cutting-edge technology within. The station served as the terminus for railways of southwestern France until 1939, after which its short platforms became unsuitable for the longer trains being used for mainline services. Post-1939, it was used for suburban services, and part of it served as a mailing center during World War II. The building was also found to be used as a film set and a temporary theater space.

In the 1970s, a plan to demolish the station was halted by Jacques Duhamel, Minister for Cultural Affairs, who instead listed the station as a Historic Monument. This decision paved the way for the station's transformation into a museum. The idea for the museum, proposed by the Directorate of the Museum of France, was to create a space that bridged the gap between the Louvre and the National Museum of Modern Art at the Georges Pompidou Centre. Georges Pompidou accepted this plan, and the Musée d'Orsay was established in 1986.

The Musée d'Orsay's collection and unique architectural history make it a significant cultural and historical landmark in Paris. Its transformation from a railway station to a museum symbolizes a blend of historical preservation and

cultural innovation, offering visitors a rich experience of French art and history.

Lunch

If you want to skip the sandwiches, the museum has a lovely lunch place. It is not expensive and is one of the stops I will visit next. musee-orsay.fr/ They even have a fancy tea room if you want something a little nicer and would love high tea. Menus were available on the link. We did not take part, but we thought about it. It was a very tempting cafe.

We skipped lunch and ran off to the Paris Catacombs, vowing to eat later at a cafe. Mom decided not to join us in the catacombs, so my daughter and I headed out independently. We would meet up afterward.

Afternoon

Paris Catacombs (not covered in the Paris Museum pass) is not as scary as I thought. There are 131 steps down (spiral staircase) and 112 going up (spiral staircase). I am certainly not as fit as I would like to be, and the upward staircase is steep, and it has to be taken at an energetic pace as people are climbing in front and behind you.

If you have claustrophobia like my mother, consider avoiding this stop entirely. Mom spent the visit in a delightful cafe, people-watching and slurping onion soup with crisp bread while I took pictures of skulls. The entire path

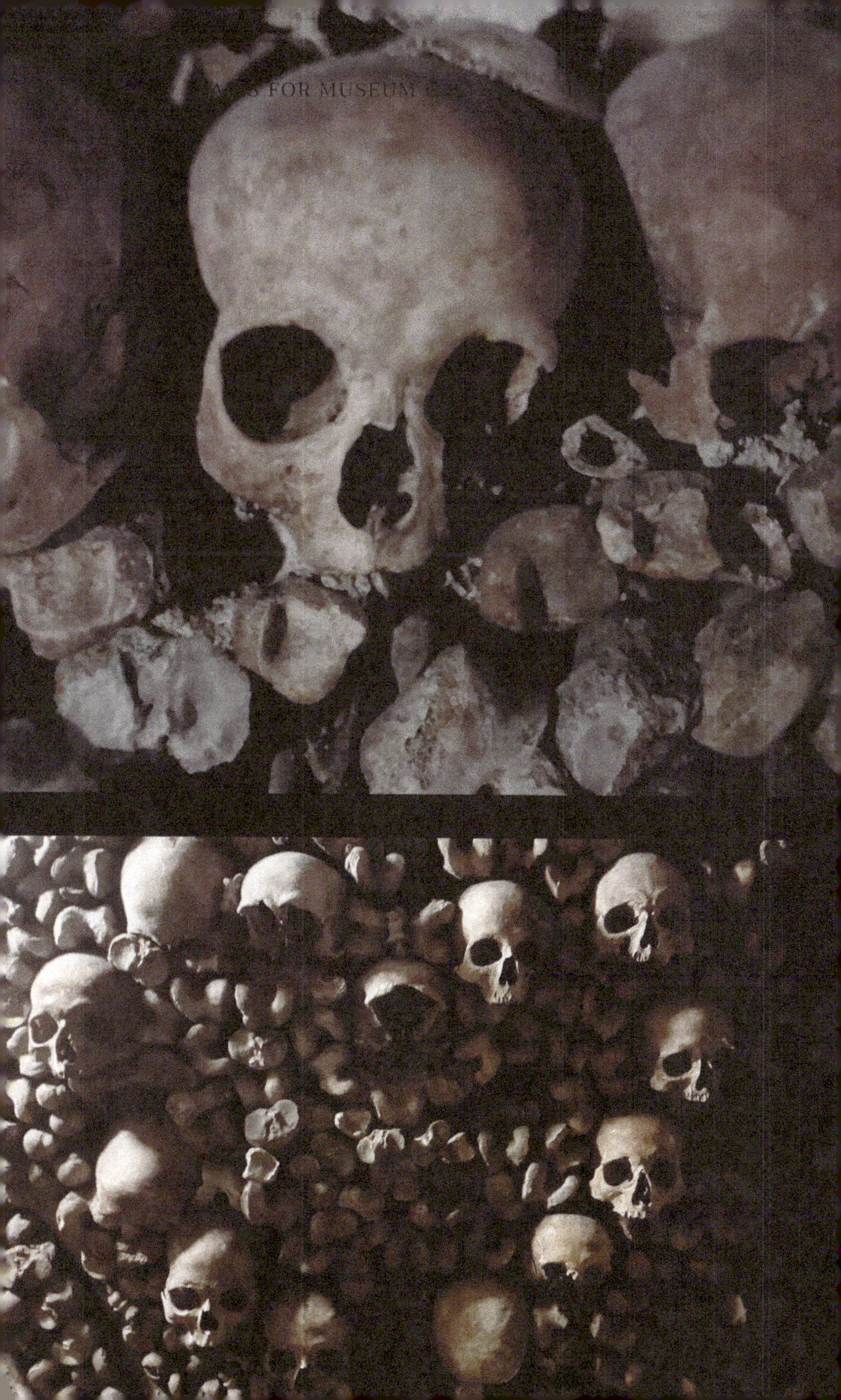

through the catacombs and the walk back to the entrance took only about an hour.

Inside, the terrain is uneven and sometimes soggy. If you have a kid who might dislike the catacombs, skip it. I would strongly advise taking the tour online on the website first to see if the kids are activated by anything in there. The entrance and exit are in different locations and require some top-side walking back to the entrance.

The history of the Paris Catacombs, a vast underground ossuary in Paris, France, begins in the late 18th century, driven by major public health concerns related to the city's overflowing cemeteries. The decision to transfer the contents of these cemeteries to an underground site was made to address these issues.

ORIGINS AND DEVELOPMENT

- **Location Choice:** For this purpose, the authorities selected the former Tombe-Issoire quarries outside the capital, under the plain of Montrouge. These quarries, part of a larger labyrinth extending under the city, had operated since at least the 15th century before being abandoned.
- **Preparation and Organization:** Charles Axel Guillaumot, an inspector at the Department of General Quarry Inspection, was tasked with preparing the site and organizing the transfer of bones. This department, established by Louis XVI in 1777, was initially founded to consolidate abandoned quarries after several ground collapses in mid-18th century Paris.

BONE TRANSFERS

- **Initial Transfers**: The first evacuations, from 1785 to 1787, focused on the Saints-Innocents cemetery, Paris's largest, which had been in use for nearly ten centuries. The bones were moved at night to avoid public and Church backlash and were deposited into quarry wells before being arranged in the galleries.
- **Continued Transfers**: Bone transfers continued after the French Revolution until 1814, targeting other Parisian cemeteries like Saint-Eustache and Saint-Nicolas-des-Champs. The process resumed in 1840 during urban renovations by Louis-Philippe and the Haussmannian reconfiguration of the city (1859-1860).

CONSECRATION AND NAMING

- **Official Consecration**: The site was consecrated as the "Paris Municipal Ossuary" on April 7, 1786, and soon adopted the name "Catacombs," inspired by the Roman catacombs.
- **Public Opening**: Starting in 1809, the Catacombs were opened by appointment, quickly becoming popular among French and foreign visitors.

HISTORICAL VISITS AND CHANGES

- **Notable Visitors**: Over the years, many illustrious individuals visited the Catacombs, including the Count of Artois (future Charles X), Austrian Emperor Francis I, and Napoleon III with his son.
- **Visiting Arrangements**: The 19th century saw various changes in visiting arrangements, from complete closure to limited openings.

The Paris Catacombs represent a unique historical and cultural site, reflecting both the practical responses to public health crises and the evolving relationship between the city of Paris and its dead. This underground ossuary is a testament to the city's rich and complex history.

Back to the hotel

Our feet were barking at us, and we did not get an Uber or taxi. We stayed true to the public transportation pledge and used trains and buses. We wanted to take the train home. Specifically, the number 6 train goes back to the Charles de Gaulle-Etoile by the Arc de Triomphe station. While I do not usually want the iconic shots in Paris, my daughter tends to want great photos. I heard all over social media that the 6 train as it crosses over the Seine is a great framed shot of the Eiffel Tower.

It was spectacular. Well worth the trip, to be sure. I must also include that the Parisians were adamant about not including their faces in the picture. Their intent was made clear using a series of gestures and my broken French. Just make sure you get close to the window when taking the picture to be clear to the riders that you want a great photo of the scenery and not of them.

Dinner

If open, the rooftop bar at the Hotel Pley is a great place to have a lightish dinner and take in the sights. Like most rooftop bars, cooperative weather and timing matter. Instead, we headed out to the Trocadero again to get even more photos of the Eiffel Tower at night and have a light dinner at Café Kleber (cafekleber.fr). It was an amazing night, though chilly; we cozied up with coffee, crepes, and lots of red wine.

We could have eaten heavier, but we were very happy to keep it light and get to bed early after taking a zillion pics on the Trocadero, watching three performance artists balancing items and one marriage proposal. It was all very fun. Just remember to watch out for scammers and pickpockets.

Chapter 22

Saturday: J'adore Dior

Who does not love a lazy Saturday morning lie-in? Not my family. I am up with the sun even when jet lagged. My mother will follow close behind, and my daughter is the last to rise, but only on demand.

Getting up early on vacation is the best part of my day because I have the city to myself. I love roaming the empty streets for hours until the world gets up. I have a steaming hot cup of coffee in one hand and my camera in the other. Some of the best photos I have ever taken were of nightgoers heading home and bakery workers starting work. It is a magical time when a city is holding its breath, waiting for the next beat.

My morning was in full swing when I realized that our favorite corner bakery, Le Pain du Faubourg, is closed on the weekends. Others were open on Saturday, but this one quickly became our favorite, with amazing bread and reasonable prices. We decided to break with our tradition and head out and grab tea and pastries while we were out.

Dior me!

Our first stop of the day was just a short bus ride away. We had to buy separate tickets, but everyone I saw online talking about this museum was thrilled with it. Ticket costs are not included in our Museum Pass. Tickets should be purchased well in advance and you choose your date and time online. The ticket cost was 12 euros.

What you will see inside is beautiful historical clothing in beautiful displays, including a light room display of ball-gowns, a smell room for perfume, and a stitching demo with two expert seamstresses showing how the dresses are constructed. Clothes range from outrageous to classic, avant-garde to chic. As you enter and leave, there is a massive wall of rainbow-colored 1/3 scale classic Dior items.

We decided to have a seat at the tearoom for breakfast. We indulged in steaming teapots and shared delightful pastries for 25 euros. But it was well worth it.

La Galerie Dior, situated at the prestigious 30 Avenue Montaigne, boasts a storied history closely linked to its founder, Christian Dior, and his distinguished successors. Christian Dior was born in 1905 in Granville, Normandy, into a family that was prosperous from their fertilizer and chemicals manufacturing business. In 1910, the Dior family relocated to Paris, maintaining their Granville villa for leisurely retreats. During the 1920s, Christian immersed himself in Paris's vibrant cultural scene, forging connections with artists and intellectuals.

In 1928, Dior embarked on a new venture, opening an art gallery with Jacques Bonjean in Paris, where they exhibited works by luminaries such as Picasso and Matisse. The 1930s brought challenges; following his mother's death and his father's business failure in 1931, Dior began selling his drawings to couture houses and worked as an illustrator for newspapers and magazines. He joined Robert Piguet as a designer in 1938. His career was briefly interrupted by military service during World War II, after which he worked for Lucien Lelong from 1941 to 1946.

The pivotal year of 1946 marked the creation of the Christian Dior couture house, a collaboration between Dior and industrialist Marcel Boussac. The house, established at 30 Avenue Montaigne, started with three ateliers and a staff of 85. Dior's first collection in 1947, known as the "New Look" revolutionized women's fashion. That same year, he founded Christian Dior Parfums, launching the iconic Miss Dior perfume. In 1948, the expansion continued with the opening of Christian Dior-New York on Fifth Avenue, offering luxury ready-to-wear and accessories.

A series of talented designers carried forward the legacy of Christian Dior. Yves Saint Laurent took the reins in 1958, followed by Marc Bohan in 1960, Gianfranco Ferré in 1989, John Galliano in 1996, Raf Simons in 2012, and Maria Grazia Chiuri in 2016. Each successor contributed their unique vision and creativity, ensuring that La Galerie Dior remained at the forefront of fashion and culture. This illustrious history reflects not just the evolution of a fashion house but also the artistic and social transformations of each era, with La Galerie Dior standing as a testament to the enduring influence and vision of Christian Dior and his successors.

Sailing the Seine

After Dior, we walked on for about ten minutes to our bus stop to take us to the Bateaux Parisiens for a one-hour cruise. We were quite far from the dock and decided to take a bus. What we did not count on was the transit labor slow down, which meant full buses were passing us by without room to board them. We ended up walking 1.4 km to the boat.

It was one of the best parts of our Paris trip. We crossed the river and walked on the left bank with the city dwellers, walking their dogs, exercising, or having small picnics with wine and cheese. I think it was the most happy and relaxed part of the trip.

We were off when we made it to the dock, in the shadow of the Eiffel Tower, and after a few minutes of waiting in a Disneyland-style line. The boat tour without food was the best option for us. I opted for the cheapest boat tour with app narration, and we paid 7.50 per ticket because we bought it with an online discount. We opted for the top of the boat because it had the best view, even if we had to endure a few drizzles and some wind. We just bundled up and snapped away at the picture. It was a wonderful time. We saw some beautiful historical buildings that we didn't have time to see on this trip. Do plan on taking a tour later if possible.

Here are the buildings you will float by:

- Les Invalides: A complex of buildings containing museums and monuments, all relating to the military history of France, as well as a hospital and a retirement home for war veterans. The Dome des Invalides houses Napoleon's tomb.

· L'Assemblée Nationale: The lower house of the French Parliament, located in the Palais Bourbon. It plays a major role in French politics and lawmaking.

· Le Musée d'Orsay: A museum housed in a former railway station, famous for its extensive collection of Impressionist and Post-Impressionist masterpieces.

· L'Institut de France: A French learned society, grouping five académies, including the Académie Française, dedicated to the arts and sciences. It manages approximately 1,000 foundations.

· La Cathédrale Notre-Dame: One of the most iconic Gothic cathedrals in the world, known for its architectural beauty and historical significance. It suffered significant damage in a 2019 fire but is undergoing restoration.

· Île Saint-Louis: A natural island in the Seine River, known for its quiet streets, quaint shops, and 17th-century architecture. It's a peaceful area with a village-like feel in the heart of Paris.

· Île de la Cité: One of two remaining natural islands in the Seine River in Paris, the site of the medieval city. It's home to Notre-Dame Cathedral and Sainte-Chapelle.

- L'Hôtel de Ville: The city hall of Paris, housing the city's local administration. It's known for its striking architecture and has been the location of the municipality of Paris since 1357.

- La Conciergerie: A former royal palace and prison in Paris, located on the Île de la Cité. It's known for its role during the Reign of Terror and as the prison of Marie Antoinette.

- Le Louvre: The world's largest art museum and a historic monument in Paris, famous for its diverse collection of art and artifacts, including the *Mona Lisa* and the *Venus de Milo*.

- La Place de la Concorde: The largest public square in Paris, known for its significant role in French history and its major landmarks, including the Luxor Obelisk and two magnificent fountains.

- Le Grand Palais: A large historic site, exhibition hall, and museum complex located at the Champs-Élysées. It's known for its grand architecture and hosts various events, exhibitions, and fairs.

When we docked again in the shadow of the Eiffel Tower, we walked through the tourists, the bracelet scammers, and donation scammers, and I am sure a fair number of pickpockets found the mulled wine booth.

By some miracle, we managed to secure a park bench, ate sandwiches, and drank wine in the shadow of the Eiffel Tower. It was magical. We opted not to pay for the 29.40 to go to the top of the Tower. It is a lovely thing to do, but I felt we got a better view from the top of the Arc de Triomphe.

We finished eating then took beautiful photos of us in front of the Tower. If you are waiting for Instagrammable photos, plenty of enterprising street vendors hold balloon bouquets of red mylar balloons, which will happily sell you a picture of yourself or your loved one holding the balloons. It is not something I would do, but the photos were cute. There is an online Instagram account that seems to be promoting this: instagram.com/photoballoonsparis. I would be very cautious about price and giving anyone your information.

Last Supper in Paris

We traipsed back up through the Jardins du Trocadéro to the bus stop to go back to the hotel to start the agonizing journey that begins with packing to leave Paris. We had become so happy here that we did not want to leave.

As we were almost back, we stopped at every store, sweetshop, and pharmacy to load up on items to take back. I don't know why I would need lollipops, but a box of 20 was purchased. Extra macarons were scooped up. A long consultation on the benefits of one face cream over another was had in earnest. I checked out about halfway through.

Dinner

We had dinner up the street at another local brasserie, La Belle Poule (recent name change to The Do Re Mi). They serve very few chicken dishes despite the restaurant's name. But they have wonderful large drinks. I did order the wonderful chicken dish. We split two desserts and 50 cL of red wine plus cocktails (labellepoule.fr/, 18 Av. Hoche, 75008 Paris).

It was the last night, and we were very sorry to go. Despite the trash strike and the transit slowdown, we had a wonderful time in Paris. We sat at the table, listing all the other places we wanted to go next time.

Top of my list was the Centre Pompidou. The Centre Pompidou, more fully the Centre National d'art et de culture Georges-Pompidou, also known as the Pompidou Centre in English, is a complex building in the Beaubourg area of the 4th arrondissement of Paris, near Les Halles, rue Montorgueil, and the Marais. The Centre Pompidou, designed by Renzo Piano and Richard Rogers, is a 20th-century architectural marvel, immediately recognizable by its exterior escalators and enormous colored tubing. It is home to the National Museum of Modern Art and is internationally renowned for its 20th and 21st-century art collections.

My daughter wanted to spend more time shopping at discount stores, and my mom wanted to spend more time at the Musee d'Orsay to dive into their impressionist collection. We all just wanted more. We want to visit again soon and seem to be planning all our trips so that we fly into and out of Paris so we can take a few extra days in the city.

Chapter 23

Sunday: Leaving Paris

As my six-day adventure in Paris draws close, I feel energized and exhausted from my museum-hopping journey. With a budget in mind, my family and I have explored some of the city's finest cultural treasures, taking in art and history from across the centuries. From the Louvre to the Musée d'Orsay and beyond, I have encountered some of the world's most beautiful and moving works of art. Yet, there is still so much more to see and do.

On my final day in Paris, we only had time to pack and get to the airport. With a mid-day flight, we had to make time to get to the airport and through security. Thankfully, we all made it on time and headed back home.

For those with more time than we had, plenty of museums and galleries exist to explore beyond the traditional tourist circuit. The Musée Rodin, for example, offers a stunning collection of sculptures, including the famous *The Thinker*. The Musée de l'Orangerie is also worth a visit, with its collection of impressionist and post-impressionist paintings by artists such as Monet and Renoir.

In addition to the museums, Paris offers a wealth of cultural experiences, from the world-renowned opera house, the Palais Garnier, to the legendary jazz clubs of Saint-Germain-des-Prés.

As my journey ends, hopefully, yours is about to start. I feel a sense of sadness at leaving behind the magic and beauty of Paris. But the memories I have made, the knowledge I have gained, and the people I have met will stay with me for a lifetime. I repeatedly return to Paris, drawn back by the vibrant culture and timeless beauty of this incredible city.

And so, as I bid farewell to Paris, I take comfort in knowing that my journey is just beginning. The world is full of wonders waiting to be explored, and my experiences in Paris will prepare me for the adventures that lie ahead. Whether traveling to new cities or simply exploring the world around me, I carry the spirit of Paris with me, always seeking out new beauty, knowledge, and experiences.

We settled into our seats, and the plane took off. I took out my travel journal and jotted down my thoughts and reflections on my time in Paris. I realize that my six-day itinerary, focused on museums and art, allowed me to delve deeper into the history and culture of the city and gave me a new appreciation for the works of art and the people who created them.

I also realize I have gained new insights into myself and the world. The art I encountered in the museums allowed me to see the world through different lenses and appreciate the beauty and complexity of the human experience. I met people from different parts of the world, learned about their cultures and perspectives, and broadened my own horizons.

As the plane touches down and I return home, I feel grateful for the opportunity to travel and experience new things. I realize that even if I cannot travel to Paris or other parts of the world, I can still find beauty and wonder in my own backyard and in the people around me.

As I step off the plane, I take a deep breath and inhale the fresh DC air. I feel rejuvenated and excited to continue exploring the world through travel, art, or personal connections. I know the lessons I learned in Paris will stay with me and guide my future journeys.

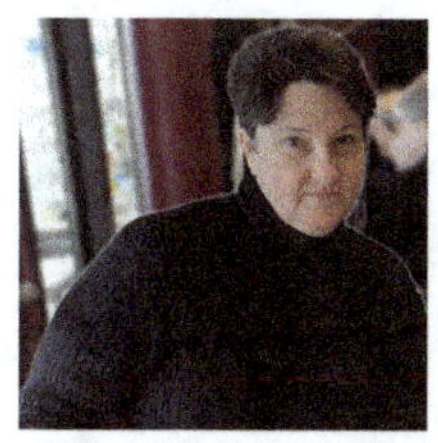

AJ Campbell is an author, playwright, and community activist living near Washington, D.C. Raised in California, her close-knit extended family would often spend their time by going to museums on the weekends and eating homemade packed lunches in the gardens. This was a cost-effective and culturally-enriching activity, as her family didn't have very much money. Amazed by the arts throughout her upbringing, she took oil painting lessons for eight or nine hours on the weekends in elementary school. One of the first paintings that struck her was *The Blue Boy* by Thomas Gainsborough circa 1770. At the time, painters would make their own paints, and the blue in the painting was incredibly remarkable to her, and almost infathomable that the ethereal shade of blue was handcrafted and expertly applied. She wondered not about the subjects of paintings but of the tireless stories of the painters and how they would stand for hours to create something from nothing. Curious about the arts and the artists behind them, she was astounded that plenty of people could paint something on a canvas, but only a tiny percentage of the population in human history might paint something that will be talked about and treasured for centuries.

More books in the Museum Lovers series are to follow, so check your local bookstore for more titles. She hopes you enjoy the arts as much as she does, and find this book helpful for your museum-filled travels to Paris and beyond.